BEST BIKE RIDES

in

NEW ENGLAND

COUNTRYMAN
TRAVELERS

BEST
BIKE RIDES
_in_
NEW ENGLAND

BACKROAD ROUTES FOR
CYCLING THE NORTHEAST STATES

DAVID SOBEL

Countryman Press

An Imprint of W. W. Norton & Company
Celebrating a Century of Independent Publishing

All photos provided by the author unless otherwise specified below:
Photography courtesy of Avi Ragaven: pages 19, 20, and 21
Photography courtesy of Chris Hardee: pages 170, 171, and 172
Photography courtesy of Jennifer Kramer: pages 50, 71, and 91
Page 97: FrankvandenBergh/iStockPhoto.com
Page 139: flySnow/iStockPhoto.com
Page 189: shunyufan/iStockPhoto.com

For information about permission to reproduce selections from this book, write to Permissions,
Countryman Press, 500 Fifth Avenue, New York, NY 10110

For information about special discounts for bulk purchases, please contact W. W. Norton
Special Sales at specialsales@wwnorton.com or 800-233-4830

Manufacturing by Versa Press
Production manager: Devon Zahn

Library of Congress Cataloging-in-Publication Data

Names: Sobel, David, 1949– author.
Title: Best bike rides in New England : backroad routes for cycling the Northeast states / David Sobel.
Description: First Edition. | New York : Countryman Press, [2023] | Series: Countryman Travelers
Identifiers: LCCN 2022028990 | ISBN 9781682687475 (Paperback) | ISBN 9781682687482 (epub)
Subjects: LCSH: Cycling—New England—Guidebooks. | Cycling—Maine—Guidebooks. |
Cycling—New Hampshire—Guidebooks. | Cycling—Vermont—Guidebooks. | Cycling—Massachusetts—
Guidebooks. | Cycling—Connecticut—Guidebooks. | Cycling—Rhode Island—Guidebooks.
Classification: LCC GV1045.5.N36 S63 2023 | DDC 796.60974—dc23/eng/20220630
LC record available at https://lccn.loc.gov/2022028990

Countryman Press
www.countrymanpress.com

An imprint of W. W. Norton & Company, Inc.
500 Fifth Avenue, New York, NY 10110
www.wwnorton.com

10 9 8 7 6 5 4 3 2 1

Frontis: LATE AFTERNOON, LOOKING WEST ACROSS CAPE COD BAY
Right: WINDOWS OF NEW ENGLAND

ONE OF THE MANY CUTS ALONG THE AIR LINE TRAIL IN EAST HAMPTON, CT

Contents

MASSACHUSETTS RIDES (West to East) | 139

CONNECTICUT RIDES (West to East) | 189

RHODE ISLAND RIDES (North to South) | 209

THE BATTLE ROAD TRAIL IN CONCORD, MA, FEELS MUCH LIKE IT MIGHT HAVE IN 1775

Rides at a Glance

Ride	Starting Point	Distance (miles)	Difficulty
1. Island Biking: North Haven, ME	Ferry parking terminal	13.5 miles	Easy/ Moderate
2. Freshwater and Saltwater: Bristol Mills, New Harbor, and Round Pond on the Pemaquid Peninsula, ME	Bristol Mills village	17.9 miles	Moderate
3. Western Maine Lakes: Waterford, Harrison, and South Waterford, ME	Gage Rice Beach Park	15.3 miles	Moderate/ Challenging
4. By the Beautiful Sea: Wells and Drakes Island, ME	Route 1 in Wells, ME	12.2 miles	Easy
5. The Sound of Music: Franconia and Sugar Hill, NH	Dow Recreational Fields	13.7 miles	Moderate/ Challenging
6. Sunny Afternoon: Lyme, NH	The NH Park and Ride lot	10.8 miles	Moderate
7. Over the Rivers and Through the Woods: Walpole, River Road, and Drewsville, NH; and Bellows Falls, VT	Behind Burdick's and the post office	25.9 miles	Challenging
8. Lost Villages Par Excellence: Lyndeborough and Davisville, NH	South Lyndeborough village on Route 31	13.5 miles	Challenging
9. Railroad Heritage: Hancock, Elmwood Junction, and Eastview, NH	Hancock Village	17.9 miles	Moderate/ Challenging
10. Land of Lakes: Chesham, Nelson, Harrisville, and Dublin, NH	Wells Memorial School	19.3 miles	Challenging
11. An Escher Ride: Westmoreland and Spofford Lake, NH	Westmoreland Town Hall	11.5 miles	Moderate
12. If You Could Choose Only One: Greensboro and East Hardwick, VT	Greensboro town parking lot	15 miles	Challenging
13. The Villages of Calais: Adamant, Maple Corner, and Kents Corner, VT	The Adamant Co-op	14.1 miles	Challenging
14. Soft Rock Mining: East Poultney and Slate Quarries, VT	East Poultney Town Green	12 miles	Moderate
15. Pleasant Valley: Saxtons River, Cambridgeport, and Brockways Mills, VT	Main Street in Saxtons River	16.4 miles	Moderate/ Challenging
16. West River Valley: Newfane and Brookline, VT	Windham County Courthouse	11.8 miles	Moderate
17. Lost Valley: Putney and Westminster West, VT	Putney Central School	12.6 miles	Moderate/ Challenging

Ride	Starting Point	Distance (miles)	Difficulty
18. Hollow and Heights: Weatherhead Hollow and Guilford Center, VT	The junction of Guilford Center Road and Weatherhead Hollow Road	12.2 miles	Challenging
19. Ashuwillticook Trail: Adams and Cheshire, MA	Adams Visitor Center	17.1 miles	Moderate
20. Old Man River and the Devil: Northfield, Gill, and Satan's Kingdom, MA	Four Stars Brewery	29.3 miles	Challenging
21. Time Travel: Turners Falls and Deerfield, MA	Great Falls Visitor Center	18.4 miles	Moderate
22. Rattlesnake Gutter: Montague and Leverett, MA	Montague Book Mill	15 miles	Challenging
23. The Hidden World of Quabbin: Petersham and Dana, MA	Quabbin Access Gate 40	14 miles	Moderate
24. Reformatory Branch and the Battle Road: Concord, Bedford, and Lexington, MA	Millbrook Tarry	15.9 miles	Easy/ Moderate
25. Back Woods and Kettle Ponds: Wellfleet and Truro, MA	Mayo Beach town parking lot	18.4 miles	Moderate
26. White Memorial Foundation: Litchfield and Bantam Lake, CT	South of Litchfield on Whites Woods Road	12.3 miles	Moderate
27. High and Low: The Air Line and East Hampton, CT	The Air Line parking area	15.1 miles	Moderate/ Challenging
28. Oh, the Places You'll Go: Mystic and Bluff Point, CT	Steamboat Wharf or the Amtrak Station	17.2 miles	Moderate
29. Blackstone River Valley National Historic Park: Lincoln Villages of Albion, Ashton, and Lime Rock, RI	Blackstone Bikeway parking area	10.1 miles	Easy
30. The Farm Coast: Adamsville and Little Compton, RI; and Acoaxet, MA	Barn Restaurant	17.2 miles	Easy

Introduction

THE GENESIS OF THE IDEA

One ride unfolds this way. First there's the climb up Hardy Hill, a narrow dirt road in a tucked away corner in the hills north of Monadnock in New Hampshire. A couple of old Capes, but mostly thick forest, the narrow road carving across the slope of the hill. Standing up in the pedals, heart thumping. At the top of the hill, at the juncture with Lead Mine Road, there's the Nelson town cemetery. Batchelders, Iselins, Parkers. Pines and oaks provide dappled shade. Moss and bluets cover the graves.

Then there's the plunge down the hill into the hilltop village of Nelson. The steepled church, the town hall of contradance fame, the tiny old Olivia Rodham library, a few well-preserved homes, a looooong train of covered mailboxes, all surrounding the gleaming green. Ridges and small peaks enclose this village vignette on the north and east. From out of the woodsy wilderness, you zoom into the well-tended protected world of a pleasantly lost village.

I arrived in Nelson for the first time on a frigid February night in 1972. We'd driven two hours from Woodford, Vermont, on narrow, ink-dark byways. As we twisted up the final steep stretch of road, not having seen a house in miles, I had serious doubts about whether my friend Stan knew where he was going. I was convinced we were lost in H. P. Lovecraft's horror story boondocks. But then, we crested the hill, cars were jammed into every available crevice in the plowed-up snow banks around the green, and the town hall shone with light and trilled with distant music. Shirt-sleeved and sweating bearded men and rosy-cheeked women stood around on the shoveled walkway outside in animated conversation.

Inside, the dance floor was packed, the music was rousing, it was humidly hot despite being 2 degrees below outside. The dance hall pulsed with life in the grip of a northern New England winter night. I felt like I'd come home. That night, I swore to myself that I would live in Nelson at some point in my life. A year later, I took up residence in a funky little cabin here. Five years later I was on the school board.

I love lost villages and old roads. It's one of the great joys of my last three decades: to poke around New England on bikes in search of historically preserved town centers, quiet dirt roads, rural corners of Connecticut, tucked-away urban pathways. I like arriving in a new town for the first time on a bike, rather than in a car, to see the way the landscape and architecture unfold. First a scattering of houses, then an old schoolhouse, then the Congregational Church and a cemetery, maybe a store. In larger ones, a pizza place and a tattoo parlor. They provide glimpses into New England history and evoke dreams of what it would be like to live here. And I like figuring out where the local swimming hole is for post-ride cleansing and renewal.

MILES OF MARSHES ALONG OLD VERNON ROAD HEADING TOWARD SATAN'S KINGDOM IN MA

This book recreates some of those explorations for you. Some of these rides are now part of our annual regimen. A few are new, recent discoveries in the constant search for perfect bike rides. (See design principles in Route Parameters on page 14.) And luckily, some of these lost villages are being found. Found enough so that there are little cafes, bakeries, bistros, and pubs tucked into restored mills and renovated opera houses. These eateries are treasures unto themselves. Take Proctorsville, Vermont, for instance. Most people zoom by on Route 103, headed to ski Okemo in nearby Ludlow, Vermont. But just a smidgeon off the road is Proctorsville, a village you didn't know existed. There's a bike ride (not in this book) that starts here at the Old Crow Bakery in the renovated opera house. Passing through the door is like entering a time warp back to 1950s Vermont, back to a Howard Frank Mosher story set in Kingdom County.

That's the idea of this book. Off the beaten track biking on back roads, rail trails, maybe some mellow single track through lost villages or hidden neighborhoods. Followed by suggestions of great places to wash away the road dust and sweat. Rounded out by lunch or an early dinner at one-of-a-kind, homegrown cafes. Bike, swim, nosh. The simple pleasures.

LOOPIFICATION

My wife and I enjoy designing new bike routes and we're always striving for good *loopification*. For instance, how do you take a section of rail trail and turn it into a loop that comes back in an interesting way? I can't stand walking out and back on the same path, or biking out and back on a trail. What a bore. A corollary of loopification is connectivity—what's the interesting way to connect different pieces on a ride, which is not necessarily the shortest distance between two points?

Therefore, this is a book of mostly 1- to 3-hour, 10- to 25-mile bike loops across New England. There are more in New Hampshire, Vermont, and Massachusetts because that's where we spend a majority of our biking time. There are equally as good ones in Maine, Connecticut, and Rhode Island as well.

This book is less for the spandex, logoed bike wear, clip-in pedals, wrap-around sunglasses crowd—the road-bikers who want to go out and pound out a fast 40 or 50 miles on a Tuesday evening ride. I feel for the stragglers pumping along a mile or two behind the pack. And though I know it'd probably be good for me, I just can't get into spin classes. Too militaristic and competitive.

Instead, I appreciate a more languid, landscape-appreciation pace. An opportunity to watch marsh transition into swamp, to glimpse old cellar holes and mill sites, to tell meandering Irish stories, taking turns back and forth, on the long climb out of Harrisville going toward Dublin village to take our minds off the climb.

I hope the rides in this book will suit a wide variety of you. There are fantastic routes here if you enjoy blending outdoor recreation with historical and natural science exploration. There are perfect rides for you and your kids to enjoy the outdoors together. The rides here are also great if you're looking to bike amiably rather than fanatically.

Mostly, this book is for you if you are interested in poking in and around the hidden corners of New England. After an afternoon of exploring when my son was about nine years old, he said, "I'm a good explorer because I really look at all the details, all the little places you can go, all the crannies you can find." Similarly, this book is about being a good explorer, finding all the off-the-beaten-path places you can go. Eons of landscape change, centuries of history, and all manner of folk art and culinary innovation weave through the landscape like the threads of fungal mycelium in soil. This book is intended to help you discover some of those crannies while your heart pumps and your smile widens. I hope it helps you appreciate the gift of life on earth.

ROUTE PARAMETERS

A lot of work has gone into refining these bike loops. Figuring out the little connector trails, using Map My Ride to get just the right topographic profile, discarding sections of road with no bike-able shoulder. For every bike ride that's in this book, there are two more waiting in the wings, serving as understudies, just not ready for prime time. They're good, but not great. All of these are great. It's worth at least $22.95 of your hard-earned cash to take advantage of all the sweat and cartographic grit we've poured into crafting these rides. Sure, you could figure them out yourself. But think of all that time you'd be wasting sitting on your butt, pounding the keyboard, when you could just be up and out the door, breezing along.

What makes these rides great? Let me articulate the design parameters.

Landscape Diversity

A good ride takes you through lots of different worlds in a short time. At the end, you're supposed to feel like, *Wow, think of all those different places we just visited.* Therefore, a good ride cruises along lakeshores, traverses marshes, has some great views from lofty vantage points, passes through a lost village, ambles along through well-maintained farm meadows. On the other hand, a ride that just drifts on and on through deep forests isn't that appealing and will more likely be buggy. For good landscape diversity, try the Rattlesnake Gutter ride in Massachusetts or the Freshwater and Saltwater ride in Maine.

Topography

There's a prototypical profile that we look for in rides. You start off flat or roll-y for the first mile or two to get warmed up. Then somewhere in the first third to half of the ride you do the long climb. Then from the halfway point to the end, you drift along level and slightly downhill. If we have a choice, we tend to choose the shorter, steeper climb earlier in the ride and the longer, shallower descent later in the ride.

Sometimes we'll refer to *wasting elevation*. This describes a descent where you waste all the hard-earned altitude you've gained by having to ride your brakes going down a too-steep hill, taking away from the carefree abandon of just letting go. The perfect profile for a short ride is illustrated in the Westmoreland and Spofford Lake ride in New Hampshire. The 2.5-mile downhill at the end, where you never have to touch your brakes, is as good as it gets. Or the downhill on Macveagh Road on the Land of Lakes ride, where you cruise through a sunlight-dappled hemlock forest and then pop out into shockingly green meadows.

Elevation Gain

We like a good workout, but we're not ardent fitness buffs. Only a few of these rides have more than a total of 1,500 feet of elevation gain. Many of them are less than 1,000 feet and a reasonable number are closer to 500 feet. We tend to avoid rides with grades over 10%; that's one foot of rise for every ten feet of run. The spectrum is illustrated in two climbs. There's the Harrisville up to Dublin Village climb of about 300 feet in 1½ miles creating a grade of 4% which is steady but reasonably mellow, suitable for conversation. On the other hand, there's the last bit of climb up to Spofford village on the Westmoreland ride that's about a 15% grade. No chatting here, but thankfully it's over pretty quickly.

We've provided topographical profiles for each ride here. And we've rated rides as:

1. Easy, with up to 500 feet of elevation gain,
2. Moderate, between 500 and 1000 feet of elevation gain
3. Challenging, more than 1000 feet of elevation gain.

If you're designing your own ride, we highly recommend using the elevation function on the Map My Ride website to preview and design possible rides.

Architectural Integrity and Lost Villages

Have you strolled along the Battle Trail in Minuteman National Historical Park in Concord? The Bloody Angle looks pretty much as it did in 1775, the old taverns and farmhouses have been restored impeccably, and even the domestic animals look like they've been regressively bred to look like the late 18th century. Though suburbia lurks just outside of your field of vision and there's a hum of traffic if you concentrate, you feel transported back in time. That's the optimal feeling for many of these bike rides. Of course, it's hard to sustain this old-time feeling, but there are swaths of New England where you can be lulled into time travel if you just blur the edges of your vision.

Perfect villages immerse you in historicity. Harrisville, New Hampshire, a national historic landmark, and Deerfield, Massachusetts, get you pretty close. Most of the buildings in Harrisville date from the 19th or early 20th century, in Deerfield from the 18th and 19th centuries. Waterford, Maine, and Maple Corner, Vermont, are similar in their integrity. Then there are the lost villages, often with just a church, a town hall, a half dozen old colonials, an old schoolhouse. You come upon these almost unexpectedly. After 40 years of living in southern New Hampshire, we finally discovered Lyndeborough Center, a classic hilltop village. And Little Compton, Rhode Island, has that similar frozen-in-time feeling.

We try to choose routes that maximize historical authenticity and tend to avoid routes that feel more mid- to late 20th century. And, of course, we prefer back roads, class 5 and 6 roads, and rail beds to busy roads and state highways. Our goal is to get behind, underneath, around the briskly traveled route. We like Old King's Highways, Mill Lanes, Poor Farm Roads, and River Roads—their names suggesting that these routes are historical remnants.

Distinctive Features

We like rides that bring you to, or by, intriguing places. These could be historical sites, one-of-a-kind museums, cool geographical features, unique stores, prime examples of New Englandiana. There's the unexpected Susan B. Anthony birthplace in Adams, Massachusetts, on the Ashuwillticook ride. Rattlesnake Gutter wins the prize for most evocative place name in New England and it's a unique geologic feature. The Book Mill in Montague, *books you don't need in a place you can't find,* is a lost village unto itself. And then there's that charming little swimming hole on one of the Walpole rides that we ferreted out one day. Or all those old one-room schoolhouses turned into residences in Guilford, Vermont. We try to choose rides that have one or more of these distinctive features along to way to poke around in.

THE INCREDIBLY CLEAR WATERS AT THE GREEN FROG SWIMMING HOLE

Bike, Swim, Dine

We're most happy when we manage the perfect trifecta of a well-designed loop, including or followed by a refreshing swim, capped off with a handcrafted meal, more often lunch, in a tucked-away cafe. It's hard to assemble all three in the same package, but that's what we've aspired to here. Easy to get two out of three on any of these rides, with sometimes a short drive to snag the third.

Therefore, each bike loop description is followed by dine and swim opportunities. The dining recommendations aren't meant to be comprehensive. That's what Trip Advisor is for. Rather I'm trying to recommend distinctive places with interesting specialties that you'd most likely overlook. We're fans of Guy Fieri's *Diners, Drive-Ins and Dives*, so you might consider this the Cafes, Bakeries, and Bistros aspect of this book. For instance, in Keene, New Hampshire, there's a dizzying array of places to nosh, but you'd probably turn up your nose at Athens Pizza on Main Street If you did, you'd miss the singularly delicious, healthy, and inexpensive Chicken Kabob plate. Or for a post ride quaff, you might miss the Hungry Diner after your Walpole and Bellows Falls ride. These dining venues have been as carefully curated as the rides.

Treasure Hunts

In keeping with the theme of poking into nooks and crannies, I've included a Treasure Hunt image for each bike ride. This is a photograph of a unique sculpture, mailbox, sign, architectural detail, interpretive plaque that is visible, but not obvious, along the way. I'll provide some clues as to where in the ride you should look. Quiet pride is the reward for finding each one.

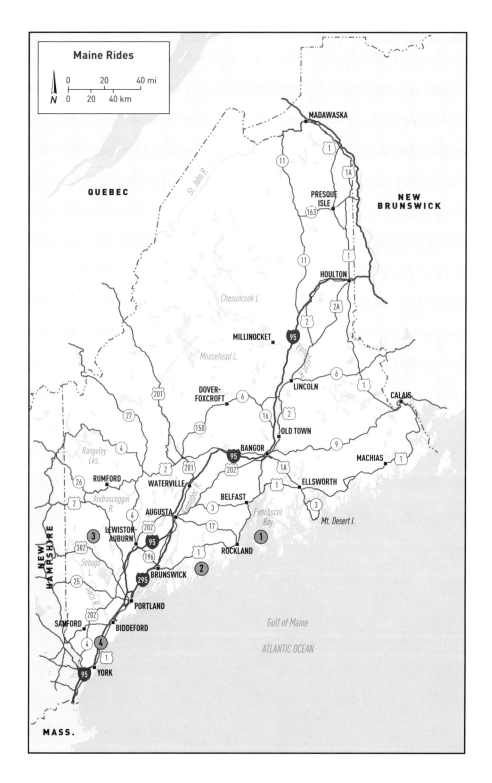

RIGHT: VIEW ACROSS PENOBSCOT BAY TO THE CAMDEN HILLS

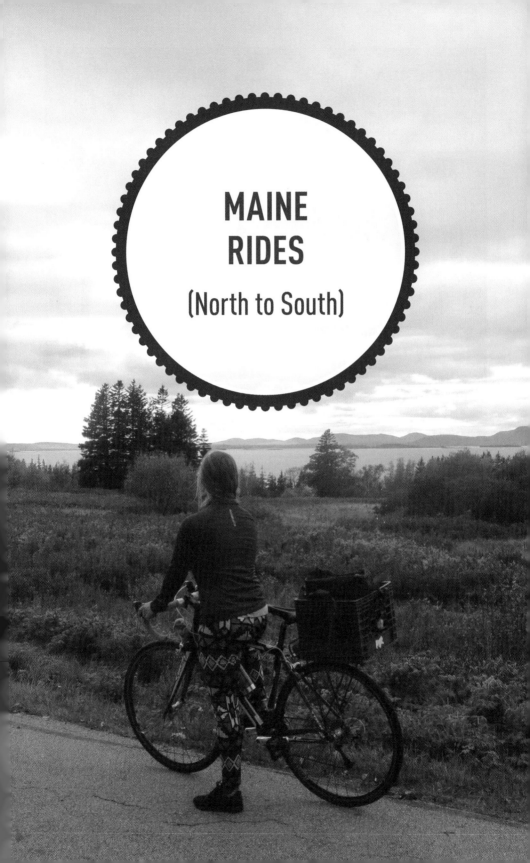

MAINE RIDES

(North to South)

BROWN'S BOATHOUSE AND WHARF AT SUNSET

1

Island Biking
North Haven, Maine

DISTANCE: 13.5 miles
ELEVATION GAIN: 618 feet
EASY/MODERATE

One of the most beautiful rides on the coast of Maine. Make a day of it, or do an overnight. A storybook village, meadows forever, and a bracing mid-ride swim spot.

Take the 9:30 ferry departing Rockland and plan to catch the 3:45 ferry departing North Haven on the way back. From late June to early September, go on Thursday, Friday, or Saturday so you can get lunch at Calderwood Hall after your ride. Be sure to allow for time before or after your ride to ramble around the village.

Start your ride from the ferry terminal parking lot. Take a left on Main Street, then a right on Mullins Lane passing the Nebo Lodge (where you will have reserved a room for the night if you're smart), then a left on Church Street and another right on Main Street. It's pretty simple from here on. After about a mile of flat cruising, bear left at the intersection onto Pulpit Harbor/School Road, and pass the K-12 North Haven Community School on your right. A wonderful school with a long commitment to community-based education. In the high school science program, they regularly rearticulate the skeletons of deceased whales. How cool is that? Past the school you come to the North Haven Grocery—your chance for picnic lunch purchases if Calderwood Hall is closed.

Continue on Pulpit Harbor/North Shore Road, descending down to cross Mill Stream. At the juncture here take a detour left to explore down to Pulpit's Harbor—maybe as far as the bridge and little beach at Norton's Cove. Gracious homes abound with lawns sprawling down to the water's edge. It's an idyllic scene; you'll be starting to think about summer rentals on this island. Turn around and head back to the intersection with North Shore Road and head north. Here's where the beauty really kicks in—mile after mile of sweeping meadows. I'm often moved to tears along here. Windswept grass, long views across Penobscot Bay to the mainland, impeccably maintained old homes—it's a vision of loveliness that most of us can't afford but can enjoy for a day or two.

After Middle Road, you'll take a left on

TREASURE HUNT: FIND THESE UNIQUE GARAGE DOORS NOT FAR PAST THE NORTH HAVEN GROCERY

Mullens Head Road toward Mullen Head Park. You'll reach a serene meadow area with lots of roads heading off in many directions and likely have it to yourself. It's possible to take a left and head down to the long beach on Banks Cove, but I prefer to bear right, stay on Mullens Head Road and look for the little pull-off and trail down to Mullen Cove. There's a pristine gravelly beach here. It's a good place for a picnic and a bask in the sun.

Back on your bike, continue south on Mullens Head Road and turn right on Indian Point Road. Beautiful tidal marshes on your left before you take a left, amidst more meadows on South Shore Road. You'll want this to last forever. At Main Street, bear left to head back into town. Don't take a left on Church Street, but rather coast down Main Street around the corner back into the village. Head for Calderwood Hall for lunch.

DINING OPPORTUNITIES

Calderwood Hall is the perfect funky and cozy island restaurant and bakery you've always dreamed about. It's run by a fleet of island women committed to healthy, local, incredibly fresh food. Good place to get a scone before your ride and lunch after. A menu that will tickle your fancy—grains and local greens bowl, fish cakes, cumin chicken, and poblano peppers pizza. And you can get locally brewed ales from the North Haven Brewery, right downstairs. Grab a Highliner Pale Ale to enjoy with your vegetarian black olives, red peppers, pickled onions, artichoke hearts, mushrooms, and feta pizza.

SWIMMING OPPORTUNITIES

Best to swim mid-ride as the swimming options near town just aren't as nice. As mentioned above, I recommend the gravelly beach at **Mullen Cove**. You'll have it to yourself, the water is impossibly clear and brisk, you'll emerge feeling pleasantly salty and glad to be alive. The sunbaked gravel is great for shaping to your body and not sticking like sand.

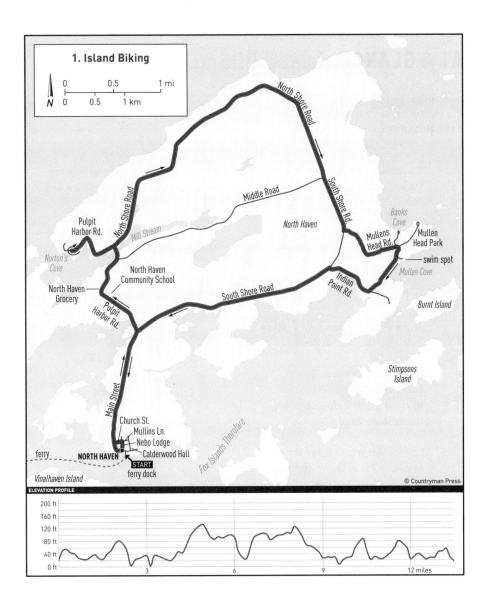

1. Island Biking

N

0   0.5   1 mi

0   0.5   1 km

Norton's Cove

Pulpit Harbor Rd.

North Shore Road

Mill Stream

North Haven Community School

North Haven Grocery

Pulpit Harbor Rd.

Main Street

North Shore Road

Middle Road

North Haven

South Shore Rd.

South Shore Road

Mullens Head Rd.

Banks Cove

Mullen Head Park

swim spot

Mullen Cove

Indian Point Rd.

Burnt Island

Stimpsons Island

Church St.

Mullins Ln.

Nebo Lodge

Calderwood Hall

ferry

NORTH HAVEN

START

ferry dock

Fox Islands Thorofare

Vinalhaven Island

© Countryman Press

ELEVATION PROFILE

200 ft
160 ft
120 ft
80 ft
40 ft
0 ft

3   6   9   12 miles

AT A GLANCE Island Biking: North Haven

DISTANCE: 13.5 miles
ELEVATION GAIN: 618 feet
EASY/MODERATE

0.0 — Disembark ferry, exit ferry parking lot, and take a left on Main Street.

0.1 — Right on Mullins Lane. Pass Nebo Lodge on right.

0.2 — Left on Church Street, then right on Main Street.

1.4 — At the V intersection, take a left on Pulpit Harbor/School Road.

2.0 — Arrive at North Haven Grocery. Last chance for picnic supplies. Bear right onto Pulpit Harbor/North Shore Road.

2.6 — Left for side trip to Pulpit Harbor. Go as far as the bridge over Norton's Cove then turn around and come back to this intersection.

3.9 — After side trip to Pulpit Harbor, head north on North Shore Road.

8.2 — Left on Mullens Head Road.

8.9 — Bear sharply right to stay on Mullens Head Road.

9.2 — Look for pull-off/side trail to Mullen Cove. Continue south on Mullens Head Road.

9.5 — Right on Indian Point Road.

10.0 — Left on South Shore Road.

12.1 — Continue straight onto Main Street. Pass Church Street and roll downtown.

13.5 — Pass Ferry Landing and turn left on Smith Street to arrive at Calderwood Hall.

2

Freshwater and Saltwater

Bristol Mills, New Harbor, and Round Pond on the Pemaquid Peninsula, Maine

DISTANCE: 17.9 miles
ELEVATION GAIN: 423 feet
MODERATE

Not completely backroads-y, but a lovely ride with all the things you want in a Maine coastal bike ride.

Start this ride in the easy-to-miss village of Bristol Mills. Most people zip by on their way from Damariscotta to Pemaquid Beach. You're going to get off of fast-trafficked Route 130 for most of this ride to the quieter side of coastal Maine. Park at the Bristol Dam turnout loop right next to The Swimming Hole above the dam in the Pemaquid River. Cool new fish ladder installed here recently.

Head south on Route 130 for just a quarter-mile, passing Upper Round Pond Road (your return route) and taking a left on Lower Round Pond Road. You'll climb a bit and then swoop down to cross the marshy Pemaquid River. Soon you'll take a right on Old County Road. You'll climb through meadows with compelling views down to the river. Exhale. As you entered Maine across the Piscataqua

ON THE LONG COVE SIDE LOOP: AS GOOD AS ACADIA WITHOUT THE TRAFFIC

TREASURE HUNT: FINE MAINE CRAFTSMANSHIP SOMEWHERE ALONG OLD COUNTY ROAD

Bridge in Portsmouth, you saw a sign that said *Welcome to Maine, The Way Life Should Be*. On Old County Road, it's the way backroads biking should be. This road rolls up and down, no serious hills, lots of old farmhouses, a few abandoned trailers and rusty cars, boats stored in dooryards. It's soothing and quiet. There are a couple of conservation areas along here providing side strolls and freshwater swim options. The forest closes in, the road turns to dirt, it feels lonely but not lost until you get to the Carpenter's Boatshop where pavement restarts and you descend to Route 130.

Time to grin and bear it for a couple miles. Lots of traffic, not very scenic, but a wide shoulder. Halfway along here you can get away from the zooming camper vans on Bradley Hill Road, a bit of old road for a quarter-mile before coming back to Route 130. After you pass the turnoff to Pemaquid Beach, the road narrows, the traffic calms, and you turn left on Route 32 to descend into New Harbor. There's a working harbor, a great dockside fish restaurant, seaweedy shores. For the next 1.5 miles, it's prime Maine coast—sun glinting off the water, waves crashing on shore. As you round the corner and see a little beach across the cove, take a mile-long detour on Long Cove Point Road. Go all the way around the loop. *Downeast Magazine* eye candy. You'll want to either buy a little cottage right here right now or at least search for summer rentals this evening in this cozy community.

Back on Route 32, you'll head north for a while. Not quite a backroad, but little traffic and a pleasing up and down lilt. You'll pass Upper Round Pond Road, your return route, and descend into a Round Pond Village. Hard to resist calling this charming. There's another working harbor here, the excellent fancy Anchor Restaurant, an ice cream stand, funky and snazzy galleries, a penny candy general store, and the made-for-bicycle-rides-stopping-point at Round Point Coffee. Croissants, a great chocolate chip cookie, iced coffee, sandwiches, a laid-back vibe. This is the place you always want to find along your rides.

Retrace your steps south back up the hill to take the right on Upper Round Pond Road. The hills are a bit bigger and swoopier here but it's only a few miles and the ride consummates with a climb to a classic farm across delicious meadows. It will take your breath away. From here it's a quick slide down into Bristol Mills, back to your parked car only a few steps from a refreshing plunge to

THE VILLAGE COFFEE SHOP YOU ALWAYS DREAM YOU'LL FIND ON YOUR RIDE

wash off the sweat from those last few climbs. Use the railing that descends into the water. The big rock is deceptively slippery.

A VIEW OF THE PROTECTED LOBSTER FISHING COVE IN NEW HARBOR

DINING OPPORTUNITIES

As suggested above, you've got to stop at **Round Pond Coffee**. I don't really like eating mid-ride, but there's great homemade, not-too-sweet lemonade and other freshly baked sweets. Or for a nostalgic taste experience, browse the penny candy at the **Granite Hall Store** or get Gifford's Ice Cream at the window around the corner.

The **Anchor Restaurant** in Round Pond comes highly recommended, though we haven't personally tried it. And **Shaw's Fish and Lobster Wharf** in New Harbor is as authentic as it gets.

SWIMMING OPPORTUNITIES

For ease of access, it's hard to beat **The Swimming Hole** right there in Bristol Mills. You'll likely have little kids and teenagers to contend with—it's a community gathering spot. Or, of course, for bracing Gulf of Maine saltwater swimming and a surprisingly un-rocky section of Maine coast, there's the glorious sweep of sand at hard-to-beat **Pemaquid Beach**.

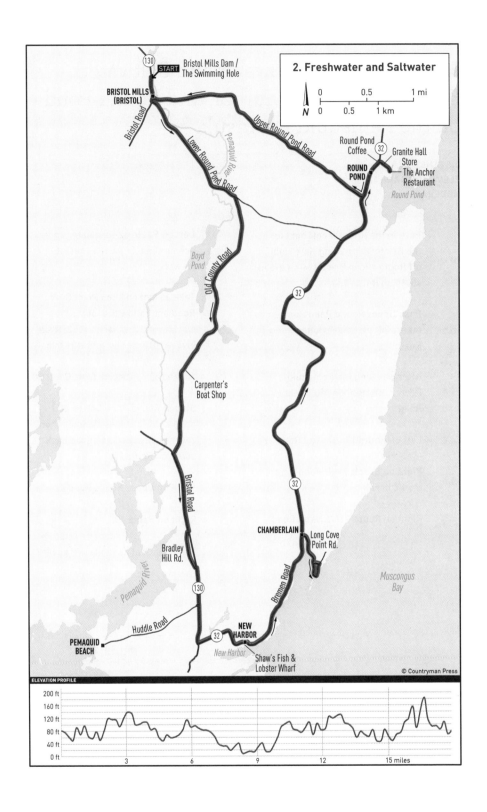

2. Freshwater and Saltwater

0   0.5   1 mi
0   0.5   1 km

Bristol Mills Dam /
The Swimming Hole

130 START

BRISTOL MILLS
(BRISTOL)

Bristol Road

Pemaquid River

Upper Round Pond Road

Lower Round Pond Road

Round Pond
Coffee

32

Granite Hall
Store

The Anchor
Restaurant

ROUND
POND

Round Pond

Boyd
Pond

Old County Road

32

Carpenter's
Boat Shop

Bristol Road

32

CHAMBERLAIN

Long Cove
Point Rd.

Bradley
Hill Rd.

Bremen Road

Muscongus
Bay

Pemaquid River

130

Huddle Road

32

NEW
HARBOR

PEMAQUID
BEACH

New Harbor

Shaw's Fish &
Lobster Wharf

© Countryman Press

ELEVATION PROFILE

200 ft
160 ft
120 ft
80 ft
40 ft
0 ft

3   6   9   12   15 miles

AT A GLANCE Freshwater and Saltwater: Bristol Mills, New Harbor, and Round Pond on the Pemaquid Peninsula

DISTANCE: 17.9 miles
ELEVATION GAIN: 423 feet
MODERATE

0.0 — Park in the little turnoff next to the Bristol Swimming Hole right off Route 130 in Bristol Mills. Head south on Route 130.

0.25 — Pass Upper Round Pond Road. and take a left on Lower Round Pond Road.

1.6 — After crossing the Pemaquid River, turn right on Old County Road.

4.6 — Left on Route 130/Bristol Road.

5.4 — Right on Bradley Hill Road for a traffic break.

5.9 — Right on Route 130/Bristol Road.

6.7 — Left on Route 32—a quieter, more scenic road. Enjoy the coastal views.

8.7 — Take a right on Long Point Cove Road and follow the loop all the way around and back to 132. It's a joyous little detour and side trip.

9.8 — Take a right back onto State Route 32.

14.6 — Stop at Round Pond Coffee and poke around in Round Pond. Then reverse direction and head back south on Route 32.

15.0 — Right on Upper Round Pond Road.

17.7 — Right on Route 130.

17.9 — Arrive back at car and take a swim.

3

Western Maine Lakes

Waterford, Harrison, and South Waterford, Maine

DISTANCE: 15.3 miles
ELEVATION GAIN: 1019 feet
MODERATE/CHALLENGING
Two lost villages, a busy little lake port, and some pleasantly lonely backroads.

This is another of those *Maine, the way biking should be* rides. Bicyclists tend to orient toward the Maine coast, but there's great biking to be had in the western Maine lake country. It's not unlike the lake worlds in the Monadnock and Winnepesaukee regions in New Hampshire. This loop brings you to and around four different lakes, all at the headwaters of the Presumpscot River, which eventually flows into the Atlantic in Portland.

Start your ride at Gage Rice Beach Park, about a half-mile east of Waterford on Route 37. There's parking for about three cars right by the beach and parking for three or four more in a little cul-de-sac just west of the beach. If you're arriving from the south and east in your car, try narrowing your vision as you pass through Waterford, so you can enter it with fresh eyes toward the end of your ride.

Saddle up and head east on Route 37 just a few tenths of a mile and bear right on Johnson Road. Climb past a nice cluster of Keoka Lake summer family cabins and take another right on Passaconaway Road. You're on a ridge between McWain Pond, which you'll never see, and Keoka. Turn right on Mill Hill Road and then left on Deer Hill Road. You'll be climbing steadily but gently along here until you top out amidst new meadows and some long views to the west. Nothing spectacular, but pleasingly quiet and remote. After about the 4-mile mark you start a long mile and a half plunge back down to lake level. It's an exhilarating, but a little bit steep, swoop.

Take a right on Route 117 and cruise along the shores of pretty Crystal Lake. This is a heavily trafficked road, but there's a good shoulder, good views, and it's slightly downhill—a good combination to offset the traffic. As you start to enter Harrison, check out Crystal Lake Park on your right. Great small beach and recreation facilities and a hopping little concession stand in the summer. Good spot to cool off mid-ride. Cruise into Harrison and stop at the Village Tie-up, right where Bear River enters Long Lake. This is also a hopping place where lots of boaters stop to gas up and dine. Even if you only want a cold drink, you should stop and sit at an umbrella-ed table with the long view down Long Lake, which stretches 11 miles down to Naples, Maine. It's a perfect little moment of summer vacationland. And you can also trundle across the footbridge over to the Long Lake Creamery, "the most picturesque ice cream stand in New England."

Continue along Route 117 through the rest of town and then veer right onto Route 35 toward Waterford. You're

A PLACID AND HISTORIC GREEN IN WATERFORD VILLAGE

now heading back upstream toward the beginning of the watershed in Keoka Lake. You'll catch glimpses of Bear River on your left and then glimpses of the cliff face of Hawk Mountain. Just when you reach Bear Pond, you'll take a sharp left on Route 37 (passing Bear Pond Park, another nice little moment), heading south for a bit and then right on short and steep Cheevers Road. This little zigzag is intended to get you off busy Routes 35/37 and onto a back road behind Bear Pond. (Alternatively, if you don't mind the traffic, you can just stay on Routes 35/37 which prettily hug the shore of Bear Pond, but there's not much shoulder.) At the top of Cheevers Road, take a right on Bear Pond Road. Although you can sense the pond down to your right, you can't see much of it. But this road is tunneled and quiet and pleasantly flat and roll-y. Once you emerge on Sweden Road, turn right and you're treated to a nice sweep of virgin asphalt (laid down in summer 2021) as you drop down past Elm Vale Cemetery (striking entranceway) into the lost village of South Waterford.

In 1870, this village was referred to as Waterford City "for the noise and bustle brought to the town by nine mills." Located on Mill Brook between Keoka and Bear Lakes, there's a more than 100-foot drop that provided the waterpower for this surprising array of mills, including a box factory, a carriage shop, a blacksmith shop, a carding mill for wool, a tannery, a sawmill, a grist mill, and a cooper's shop. Hard to imagine this little hamlet having so much industrial fervor. Stop at the historical plaque right at the corner of Sweden Road and Routes 35/37 for a fuller picture.

Turn left on Routes 35/37 to climb back up to Keoka Lake which appears through the trees to your right. You'll follow the shore around past the town

THE ELMS ARE GONE, BUT THE ENTRYWAY IS JUST AS GRAND

TREASURE HUNT: IT USED TO BE THE MAINE HYGIENIC INSTITUTE FOR WOMEN

beach and library and then enter into the Waterford Historic District. It's no surprise that the village is on the National Register of Historic Places.

Most of the village buildings were constructed in the early 19th century. There's a beautiful church, an old general store now rehabbed as a yoga studio and residence, the community hall, and the sadly neglected Lake House. Once a tavern and the home of the Maine Hygienic Institute for Women, it was a chic country inn and restaurant in the late 20th century. (Mickey Rooney and Judy Garland slept here!) The village is clustered around a beautiful green. Relax on one of the benches and enjoy the serenity of this lost village in the dappled sunlight before jumping back on your bike for the last half-mile back to Gage Rice Beach. How fortunate to have a beautiful sandy beach and the clear waters of Keoka Lake to refresh you at the end of this ride.

DINING OPPORTUNITIES

Remember I said that a stop at the **Village Tie-Up** was required. There's a comprehensive deli menu with meatball and Reuben sandwiches, soups, and salads. I confess, we had a steak bomb with all the trimmings. Stick-to-your-ribs, indulgent food. But if only to get a cold Nantucket Nectar Kiwi Strawberry, you'll enjoy sitting at the umbrella-ed table with the long view down Long Lake. Or, for your sweet tooth, you can stroll across the footbridge to the **Lakeside Creamery**.

If you're heading north, stop at the **Melby's Market and Eatery** in North Waterford. One Trip Advisor reviewer said, "This is THE classic Maine country store/diner. It's old and funky and simple and definitely has that 'good old days' vibe. If you were to conjure up an image of a no-nonsense, rural, middle-of-nowhere store where the booths and counter look like something out of a 1950s movie, then this is the place." Sounds like another time warp opportunity to me.

SWIMMING OPPORTUNITIES:

Your starting and ending point is **Gage Rice Beach**, located just east of Waterford on Route 37. The beach is sandy and shallow, the water clear, and though it's right on the road it feels quiet and protected.

Back before entering the village of Waterford, you passed the more prominent **Waterford Town Beach** on your right. More parking here and it's a little less private, but it's just as sandy and the water is just as inviting.

ANOTHER RIDE NEARBY: BOLSTER MILLS AND SCRIBNER MILL

DISTANCE: 14.5 miles
ELEVATION GAIN: 775 feet
MODERATE
An interesting foray into off-the-beaten-path rural Maine. One lost village, a surprising historical site, beautiful high meadows, and then a rollercoaster ride.

Park on Route 117, 5.3 miles east of Harrison, after crossing the Crooked River at either the fishing access or land trust parking areas on the south side of the road. South on Plains Road to Bolsters Mills. Continue south on Bolsters Mill Road to a right on Jesse Mill Road. Arrive at Scribner Mill and continue west on Scribner's Mill Road. Right on Maple Ridge Road. Right on Haskell Hill Road. Left on Bolsters Mills Road. Right on Route 117 and back to car.

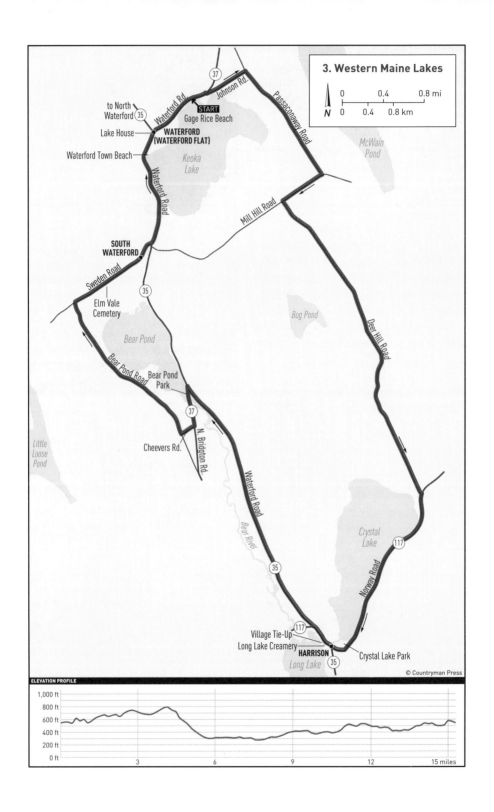

3. Western Maine Lakes

0   0.4   0.8 mi
0   0.4   0.8 km

N

37

to North Waterford   35

Johnson Rd.

Waterford Rd.

Passaconaway Road

START
Gage Rice Beach

Lake House
WATERFORD
(WATERFORD FLAT)

McWain Pond

Waterford Town Beach

Keoka Lake

Waterford Road

Mill Hill Road

SOUTH WATERFORD

Sweden Road

35

Elm Vale Cemetery

Bog Pond

Deer Hill Road

Bear Pond

Bear Pond Road

Bear Pond Park

Little Loose Pond

37

Cheevers Rd.

N. Bridgton Rd.

Waterford Road

Bear River

Crystal Lake

35

117

Norway Road

Village Tie-Up
Long Lake Creamery

117

HARRISON

Crystal Lake Park

Long Lake   35

© Countryman Press

ELEVATION PROFILE

1,000 ft				
800 ft				
600 ft				
400 ft				
200 ft				
0 ft	3	6	9	12	15 miles

AT A GLANCE Western Maine Lakes: Waterford, Harrison, and South Waterford

DISTANCE: 15.3 miles
ELEVATION GAIN: 1019 feet
MODERATE/CHALLENGING

0.0 Park at Gage Rice Beach just northeast of Waterford village on Route 37. Two different small areas to park in. Head east on Route 37.

0.2 Bear right, off of Route 37 onto Johnson Road.

0.6 Right on Passaconaway Road.

1.9 Right on Mill Hill Road.

2.4 Left on Deer Hill Road. Climb for 2 miles and then swoop down to Crystal Lake.

5.7 Turn right onto Route 117/Norway Road.

7.6 Requisite stop at Village Tie-Up. Continue on Route 117.

7.8 Bear right on Route 35/Waterford Road.

10.5 Left on Route 37 heading south for just a bit.

10.9 Right on Cheevers Road.

11.0 Right on Bear Pond Road.

12.7 Right on Sweden Road. Dally through the lost village of South Waterford.

13.7 Left on Routes 35/37/Waterford Road.

14.8 Dally in Waterford Historic District. Then at junction of Routes 35 and 37, bear right on Route 37.

15.3 Arrive at Gage Rice Beach.

4

By the Beautiful Sea

Wells and Drakes Island, Maine

DISTANCE: 12.2 miles
ELEVATION GAIN: 434 feet
EASY

Not a glamorous ride, but an interesting ride in an unexpected place. Escape Route 1 in commercialized southern Maine and travel on quiet back roads. Knock around a cozy, salt-marsh-surrounded, summer vacation neighborhood. Ride your bike on the beach!

Start your ride on Route 1 in Wells, Maine. The Post Office is one possibility. I like large, mostly unused parking lots at commercial buildings. For this ride, we'll start at the parking lot for Choice Furniture and the Bitter End restaurant (2118 Post Road) on the west side of Route 1, just north of Drakes Island Road. Other lots right around here will do if this one is crowded.

The trick in southern Maine, meaning north of Kittery and south of Portland, is avoiding heavily trafficked Routes 1 and 9. It's also hard to find loops because so many roads head out onto peninsulas and then dead-end. And though it's wonderful that the Rachel Carson National Wildlife Refuge has preserved much of the coastal salt marshes and estuaries, you can't bike the roads and trails on those properties. This ride provides a smorgasbord of southern Maine bike

THE CAUSEWAY ACROSS THE SALT MARSH TO DRAKES ISLAND

A NEW ENGLAND RARITY—A BEACH FIRM ENOUGH TO BIKE ON

riding—quiet but paved backroads, salt marsh expanses, a glimpse of summer vacationland, just a bit of heavily commercialized Route 1, and the opportunity to ride your bike on the beach. A little bit of everything.

Head north on busy Route 1 and take your first left on Coles Hill Road. You're quickly away from traffic buzz and into shady rural burbs. The road crosses the pretty Merriland River, then climbs steadily past some expansive meadows and crosses over the Maine Turnpike. Take a sharp left on Mildram Road and pass a beautiful old farm/antique store. This now feels like good old Maine countryside. Left on Route 9A. Nothing very interesting along here, but the shoulder is pleasingly wide. You'll soon get to the Wells Parks and Recreation Department facility on the right—a good alternative

starting point for the ride. You will turn left on Burnt Mill Road for a long, slow descent back to Route 1, where you take a left. If you're into browsing for old furniture, this strip is antiquing heaven.

Just before mile 8, take a right on Drakes Island Road and cruise through the salt marshes of the Wells National Estuarine Reserve. Just at the beginning of Drakes Island, take a right on Shady Lane. Keep taking rights until you make it out to the entrance to the parking area. Don't enter, but follow instead a short lane down to the right to a beautiful bay beach on Wells Harbor. Wonderful out-of-the-way bay swimming spot at high tide. Retrace your steps and bear right on Island Beach Road, past beach houses galore. You'd be happy if you owned any one of these. Pass the main beach access (tiny parking lot) and continue north to the end of the road where the houses get even glitzier. At the end, bear left until you get to the stone gate trail entrance to Laudholm Farm/Wells Reserve. No biking past here, but it's fun to stroll up into this beautifully maintained landscape.

Now the fun part. If you're into some beach riding (impossible on most New England beaches), walk your bike across the beach boardwalk, over the stones, and head down to the wide expanse of packed and exposed sand. (This only works at mid to low tides.) Ride back to the main beach access point, or if you're enjoying this unique experience, head all the way down to the stone jetty and exit via the far parking lot. In these directions, I'm assuming you'll exit at the access point at the middle of the beach. Walk your bike through the un-ride-able sand and get back onto Drakes Island Road. Pass the sensuous saltmarshes once again as you head back up to Route 1. Take a right and you're back at your car.

DINING OPPORTUNITIES

No better place for lunch and an IPA than the **Bitter End**, right where your car is parked. This small restaurant manages to transport you far away from the rush of Route 1 in just a few short steps back into their sequestered outdoor dining and bar area. Almost feels like you're at the seaside. If you indulge in fried food, try the onion strings, but make sure you have someone to share them with. And, as an aficionado of clam chowder, I can recommend this one highly. If you haven't had a Maine Lunch brewed by the Maine Brewing Company in Freeport, treat yourself. This is really one of the most delicious IPAs in New England. Pricey, but worth it.

If ice cream is your thing, I recommend the **Scoop Deck**, about 3 miles south on Route 1. Often crowded, but the line moves fast. A small scoop of the Almond Joy will do the trick.

TREASURE HUNT: A MINI-STONEHENGE SOMEWHERE ON DRAKES ISLAND

SWIMMING OPPORTUNITIES

Hard to find a better swim option on the southern Maine coast than **Drakes Island Beach**. There are two pay-to-park lots, one just as you get to the island, the other at the far southern end of the island. On weekends, these lots fill up fast, like, by 11. And then there's no other option and Wells police patrol for illegally parked cars. Of course, if you arrive by bike, that's not a problem. Since parking is limited, the beach doesn't get super crowded and if you head down toward the Wells Reserve end, you'll have more space. The body surfing is often perfect on this beach. Just the right size waves, soft sand, a long outrun. You'll feel like a kid again. At the southern end, on the bay side which you stopped at before, is a beautifully protected little beach—nice at high tides.

ANOTHER RIDE NEARBY: KENNEBUNKPORT BEACHES

DISTANCE: 15.3 miles
ELEVATION GAIN: 400 feet
LEVEL: Easy
For a grander coastal ride with giant estates (The Bush Compound) and hotels and lots more coastline and lots more traffic, consider this loop.

Start in Kennebunkport. Ocean Drive and Shore Drive and Wildes District Road to Cape Porpoise. Then south on Route 9 to Old Cape Road to Town House Corners. Arundel Road to Durrell's Bridge Road to Route 35 to Heath Road to Sea Road. Cross Route 9. Sea Road to Beach Road and back into Kennebunkport.

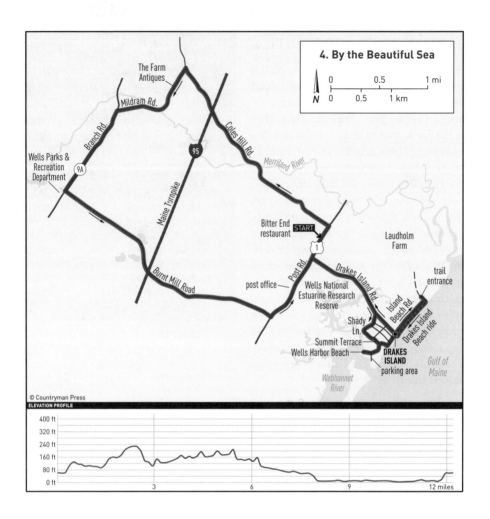

4. By the Beautiful Sea

The Farm Antiques

Mildram Rd.

Branch Rd.

Coles Hill Rd.

Merriland River

95

Wells Parks & Recreation Department

9A

Maine Turnpike

Bitter End restaurant   START

1

Laudholm Farm

trail entrance

Burnt Mill Road

post office   Post Rd.   Drakes Island Rd.

Wells National Estuarine Research Reserve

Island Beach Rd.

Shady Ln.

Drakes Island Beach ride

Summit Terrace

Wells Harbor Beach

DRAKES ISLAND parking area

Gulf of Maine

Webhannet River

© Countryman Press

ELEVATION PROFILE

400 ft			
320 ft			
240 ft			
160 ft			
80 ft			
0 ft	3	6	9	12 miles

AT A GLANCE By the Beautiful Sea: Wells and Drakes Island

DISTANCE: 12.2 miles
ELEVATION GAIN: 434 feet
EASY

0.0   Park at 2118 Post Road/Route 1 in the lot between the Bitter End and Choice Furniture. Head north on Route 1.

0.2   Left on Coles Hill Road.

2.5   Left on Mildram Road.

3.4   Left on Route 9A/Branch Road.

4.4   Left on Burnt Mill Road.

7.1   Left on Route 1/Post Road.

7.8   Right on Drakes Island Road.

8.8   Right on Shady Lane.

9.1   Continue straight onto Summit Terrace.

9.2   Right onto Island Beach Road. and find your way to the end of the lane on Wells Harbor and . . .

9.4   Arrive at Wells Harbor Beach. Retrace steps back to . . .

9.6   Bear right on Island Beach Road and follow it to end at . . .

10.4   the Gate to Laudholm Farm/Wells Reserve trail. Turn around and follow the boardwalk out onto the beach.

10.5   Ride south on the beach. Whoopee!

10.9   Exit beach onto Drakes Island Road and continue straight.

12.1   Right on Route 1.

12.3   Arrive back at car.

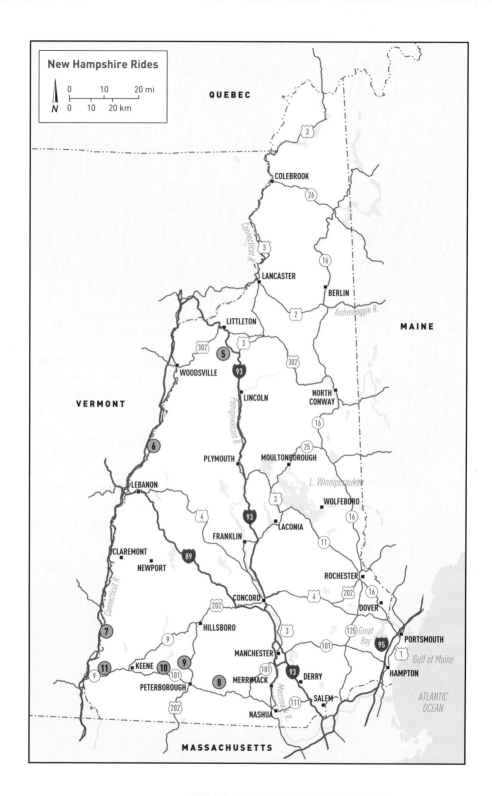

New Hampshire Rides

0   10   20 mi
0 10 20 km

N

QUEBEC

COLEBROOK
26
3

Connecticut R.
3
16
LANCASTER
BERLIN
Androscoggin R.
2

MAINE

LITTLETON
302   3
5
WOODSVILLE   93
LINCOLN   NORTH CONWAY
302

VERMONT

Pemigewasset R.
16
25
6
PLYMOUTH   MOULTONBOROUGH
L. Winnipesaukee
LEBANON   3   WOLFEBORO
4   93   16
FRANKLIN   LACONIA
11
CLAREMONT   89
NEWPORT
ROCHESTER
202   16
Connecticut R.   4   DOVER
CONCORD
202   3
7   HILLSBORO   125 Great Bay   PORTSMOUTH
9   101   95   1
11   KEENE   10   9   MANCHESTER   Gulf of Maine
9   101   101   HAMPTON
8   MERRIMACK   93   DERRY
PETERBOROUGH   SALEM   ATLANTIC OCEAN
111
202   NASHUA   Merrimack R.

MASSACHUSETTS

RIGHT: DAYLILIES AND SUGAR MAPLES ALONG LOVER'S LANE IN SUGAR HILL

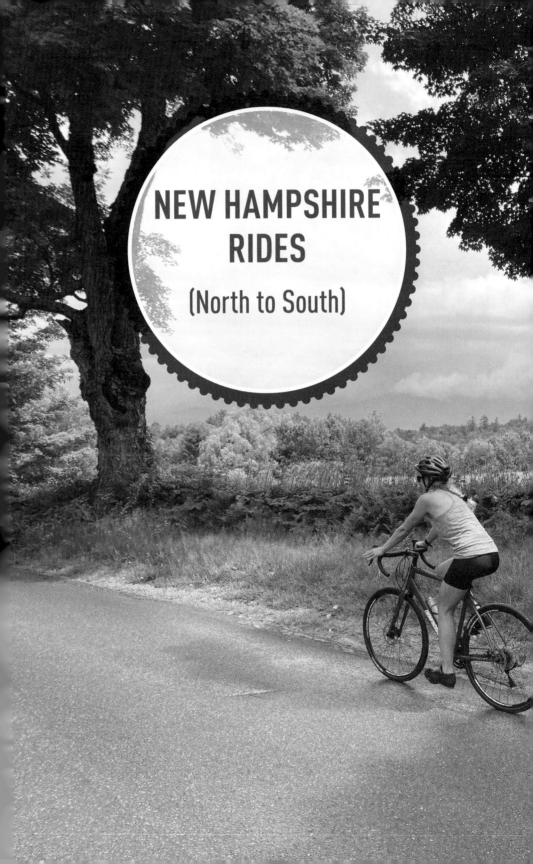

NEW HAMPSHIRE RIDES

(North to South)

TAKING A BREATHER AT THE SUGAR HILL COMMUNITY CHURCH

5

The Sound of Music

Franconia and Sugar Hill, New Hampshire

DISTANCE: 13.7 miles
ELEVATION GAIN: 905 feet
MODERATE/CHALLENGING
A wows-ville ride with stunning mountain views and a visit to one of New Hampshire's storybook lost villages. The long climb is worth it.

Park for this ride at the Dow Recreational Fields on Academy Street in Franconia, just off of Route 116. Franconia is not a lost village, due to its location right at an offramp exit from I-93. But it's the worldwide headquarters for Garnet Hill, is close to Cannon Mountain, has a good downtown market, and a host of great places to stay tucked back in the woods.

At the end of Academy Road, take a left, heading south on Route 116/Easton Valley Road. Make friends with this road—you're on it for more than 5 miles. It's not a backroad, but it's reasonably untrafficked and the views of the back side of Cannon Mountain and the Kinsman range are eye-popping. Ride the serviceable shoulder as the road follows the Ham Branch of the Gale River. After a

MARSH AND KINSMAN RANGE VIEWS ALONG EASTON ROAD

TREASURE HUNT: EASY TO FIGURE OUT WHERE YOU'LL FIND THIS.

couple of miles, you'll pass the Franconia Airport, home of the very active Franconia Soaring Association, where you can take a ride in an unpowered glider after being towed up to altitude. A great post-ride option? And the airport is located right across from the cozy Franconia Inn, which has an excellent network of Nordic ski trails during the non-biking season.

After the airport, Route 116 gets somewhat rollier, with some short climbs and descents. Eventually, you'll take a right on Sugar Hill Road. You'll be climbing for the next 4 miles. Thankfully, it's never that steep, and the total elevation gain is only about 500 feet, so it's doable. The climb happens in two steps. During the first step, you're passing lots of new construction ski vacation homes. Another couple of miles and you'll take a right on Dyke Road for a quick plummet down

into the valley of Salmon Hole Brook, and then you'll take a quick left on Easton Road. This second climb is gentler and graced with old farms—you'll start to get that biking-back-into-history feeling. At Sunnyside Cemetery, take a right on Route 117 and climb into the mildly lost village of Sugar Hill. The lawns are remarkably manicured, the gardens are well-tended, and there's the tiny post office and the historical society and the problematically named Caroline Crapo Memorial Hall.

A stop at Harman's Cheese and Country Store is de rigeur. It's the general store from your favorite childhood storybook. Try the cheese samples on the front porch—the sun-warmed nibbles of the three-year-aged cheddar are tart and full-bodied. Wash it down with some effervescent maple sap soda. And wonder what the ladies sitting in the chairs in front of the Historical Society across the street are chatting about. We sat out a 20-minute rain shower here in the shade of the porch geraniums and mellowed in the ambiance.

Resume your ride, climbing up 117 to the Community Church at the junction with Lover's Lane. My recommendation is to take a left here on this quiet back road. But that means you miss some of the really spectacular views Sugar Hill is known for. So consider this detour:

Detour: Continue the climb on Route 117, and take a right on Sunset Hill Road. Pass by the classic summer homes and hotels and make it as far as the Observation Deck, about 0.4 miles. It's particularly breathtaking during autumn sunsets, but it's pretty darn breathtaking any time. From here you can return back to the Community Church and take Lover's Lane, or you can take a right on Route 117 and begin your descent into Franconia.

From the Community Church, take the left and start with a forested descent followed by a climb through hidden meadows. The disadvantage of Lover's Lane is that there are about three of these quick up and downs. The advantage is that you're off the busier road and this backroad is really lovely. Stately homes, weathered barns, views almost as grand as from the main road. Plunge down to Route 117, take a left, and then enjoy the fruits of all that earlier climbing with a swoop down into the valley. The road surface is a bit too rough to let go completely, but you'll feel the joie de vivre of being alive in the mountains.

At the bottom of the swoop take a right on Route 18/Profile Road. Pass Garnet Hill and lots of shops, take a right on Route 116/

Easton Valley Road, and you're back where you started.

DINING OPPORTUNITIES

Franconia Market and Deli. It's not charming, but it's well-provisioned, and we got a great picnic lunch to eat at the swimming hole after our ride. Excellent chicken salad and turkey sandwiches.

Polly's Pancake Parlor is one of those big, touristy places back up in Sugar Hill. You passed it if you stayed on Route 117 from the top, and you missed it if you went on Lover's Lane. Open from 7 a.m. to 3 p.m. I'm not a big fan of carb-laden pancakes and waffles, but folks rave about this place *(best pancakes in the world!)*, and they've got an extensive menu of all kinds of breakfast and lunch options.

Schilling Beer Company is becoming the go-to brewery in Littleton. We always enjoy a cold IPA after a ride. Schilling has a hard-to-beat location, right by the Ammonusuc in downtown Littleton. Great view of the rapids. The Combover IPA is the perfect bright, citrusy quaff after a ride. Good pizza and great food truck with sumptuous smash burgers.

SWIMMING OPPORTUNITY

Green Frog is a modest, but nearby, swimming (well, actually, dipping) spot on the Gale River right near the end of this ride. Take Route 18/Profile Road about a half-mile east toward Cannon Mountain. At the junction with Route 142/Forest Hill Road, there's a well-defined gravel pullover on your right. At the corner of the parking area, there's a trailhead sign for a trail down to Green Frog—about 100 yards. It's only about waist-deep, but it's private, the water is sparkly clear, and it's a great picnic spot.

AUTHOR AND FREDO VIE FOR A STICK IN GREEN FROG SWIMMING HOLE

For more of a real swim, there's **Echo Lake**, right up past Cannon Mountain. It's a New Hampshire State Park, you have to pay admission, and it can be crowded. But it really is a fantastic swim spot with drop-dead gorgeous views of Franconia Notch. I cast my normal avoid-tourist-spots-aversion to the wind to enjoy refreshingly brisk swims here.

OTHER RECREATIONAL OPPORTUNITIES

Another bike ride to consider is the **Franconia Notch Bike Trail**. It's mostly downhill, but be prepared for some uphill, and it's a mellow roller-coaster of a ride. You can't beat the views, and there are umpteen great swim spots along the way. One of the best bike trails in New England. I recommend doing it one way. Arrange a shuttle to pick you up at The Flume and take you back to your parked car.

If you want to follow up your ride with some time on top of the water, consider a half-day or full-day outing with **North Country Kayak**. (Full disclosure: Eli Sobel, the proprietor and guide, is my son.) There are great flatwater and quickwater paddling opportunities all around this area on Echo Lake, Moore Reservoir, Long Pond, the Androscoggin, and the Pemigewasset. You can take a guided tour or rent single or tandem kayaks. Eli provides a great mix of recreation, natural history, and charm.

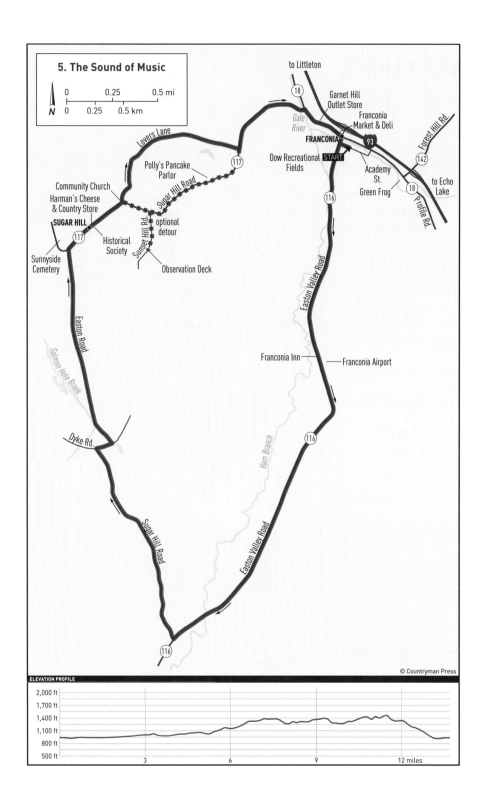

5. The Sound of Music

0   0.25   0.5 mi
0   0.25 0.5 km
N

to Littleton

18

Garnet Hill
Outlet Store

Gale
River

Franconia
Market & Deli

FRANCONIA

93

Forest Hill Rd.

Lovers Lane

Polly's Pancake
Parlor

117

Dow Recreational START
Fields

142

Community Church

Sugar Hill Road

Academy
St.

Green Frog

18

to Echo
Lake

Harman's Cheese
& Country Store

SUGAR HILL

117

optional
detour

Sunset Hill Rd.

116

Profile Rd.

Historical
Society

Sunnyside
Cemetery

Observation Deck

Easton Road

Easton Valley Road

Salmon Hole Brook

Franconia Inn

Franconia Airport

Dyke Rd.

116

Ham Branch

Sugar Hill Road

Easton Valley Road

116

© Countryman Press

ELEVATION PROFILE

2,000 ft				
1,700 ft				
1,400 ft				
1,100 ft				
800 ft				
500 ft	3	6	9	12 miles

AT A GLANCE The Sound of Music: Franconia and Sugar Hill

DISTANCE: 13.7 miles
ELEVATION GAIN: 905 feet
MODERATE/CHALLENGING

0.0 Park at Dow Recreational Fields just off Route 116 in Franconia. Turn left and head south on Route 116.

5.6 Turn right on Sugar Hill Road.

7.7 Right on Dyke Road for a quick plunge.

7.9 Left on Easton Road.

9.9 Right on Route 117.

10.2 Compulsory stop at Harman's Cheese and Country Store.

10.6 Left on Lover's Lane.

Optional detour—*Continue 0.3 miles on Route 117, turn right on Sunset Hill Road, then travel 0.4 miles to Observation Deck. Retrace your steps on Sunset Hill and either return left to Lover's Lane or turn right on Route 117 to start your descent to Franconia.*

12.3 Turn left on Route 117 and soar down into Franconia.

13.2 Turn right on Route 18/Profile Road.

13.7 Turn right on Route 116 and then left on Academy Road.

6

Sunny Afternoon

Lyme, New Hampshire

DISTANCE: 10.8 miles
ELEVATION GAIN: 756 feet
MODERATE

A totally delightful experience. Supremely quiet, bucolic, great river and ridge-top views. It's short, but it's a rough-cut gem.

Start this ride at the NH Park and Ride lot in the center of pastoral Lyme, New Hampshire, a good counterpoint to bustling Hanover, 10 miles south. The lot is right off the green and faces Matt Brown's print shop. If his shop is, perchance, open, you have to stop in. We're big fans of his place-based lithographic prints which capture the sublime beauty of the New Hampshire mountains, the Maine coast, and lots of other places. One of his moonlight-on-an-island prints graces our entrance hallway.

Connecticut River Valley rides are a staple of our bike repertoire. There are River Road rides all up and down both sides of the river from Connecticut up to northern New Hampshire and Vermont. And though you expect these rides to be flat, they often plunge in and out of stream valleys descending from the hills, which makes them rollier than you'd anticipate. This ride is comfortably flat with a couple of healthy hills thrown in.

One of the challenges with River Road rides is figuring out how to loop-ify them (i.e., make a nice out-and-back loop) without getting stuck on trafficky state highways part of the time—Route 5 on the Vermont side and Route 10 on the New Hampshire side. This ride mostly solves that problem with a few busy roads at the beginning and end of the ride. But the middle two-thirds are so gosh-darn delightful that it's worth the bothersome parts.

Head west from the village on the East Thetford Road, rolling through beautiful meadows, and then swoop down to turn right onto River Road just before the Lyme-East Thetford bridge. The next 4 miles are unfettered bliss. Sometimes you're above the river, sometimes right down on the banks. You alternate between goldfinch-brightened meadows and shadowed maple leaf tunnels. The houses and farms are mostly

TURN RIGHT ON RIVER ROAD BEFORE CROSSING THE
LYME-EAST THETFORD BRIDGE

VIEW OF THE RIVER AND VERMONT HILLS FROM RIVER ROAD

19th-century vintage. It's the river road of your dreams. Just before reaching Clay Brook, turn uphill on Breck Hill Road. Yes, any road with "hill" in its name foretells a climb. The first chunk is steep—13%—but it doesn't last that long, and then you're on an open-vista-ed north/south ridge with views to the Connecticut River Valley on the east and the Clay Brook Valley on the west. Completely serene. There's another short steep climb and then you descend to take a left on the North Thetford Road. Paved now, less private, but still serene.

Eventually, you take a right on Route 10/Dartmouth College Highway. Grin and bear it. You'll soon pass Post Pond. Turn right down the access road to check out the boat landing as a post-ride swim spot. Then continue south to pass Loch Lyme Lodge on the right with its appealing grassy meadows-down-to-the-pond family recreation area. After the pond, there's a steady, mildly unpleasant climb with a skimpy shoulder and cars whizzing past. There's an explorable cemetery right as you start to enter the village. Find the gravestones near the road with residents who relocated from Keene, New Hampshire, and Provincetown, Massachusetts-two of our other favorite bike destinations.

At the fork by the Congregational Church, bear left and cross Dorchester Road and turn right on On the Common Road to bring you back to your car.

DINING OPPORTUNITIES

Thank your lucky stars that you're parked right next to a fantastic lunch or dinner destination. **Stella's Italian Kitchen and Market** couldn't be more sumptuous. Last time we were there I had a grilled pastrami, Swiss, and sauerkraut sandwich that was to die for. The crispy eggplant with peppers, pickled onions,

TREASURE HUNT: FIND HENRY CARPENTER'S HEADSTONE IN THE CEMETERY RIGHT BEFORE ENTERING THE VILLAGE AT THE END OF THE RIDE

and feta looked similarly appealing. No reason to search any further than where you have landed. Full dinner menu as well if you're there at the end of the day. Though we tend to bemoan the fact that the Vermont dining scene is more appealing than the New Hampshire scene, this place is an exception to that rule.

SWIMMING OPPORTUNITIES

You stopped in at the boat ramp on **Post Pond**. This is a fine swim spot. The Lyme town beach is adjacent but the sign says you need a sticker. When we were just here, a young woman confessed that she had just been chastised for washing her dog in the shallow water with Dr. Bronner's and baking soda. Two swimmers had called her a "terrible person" for polluting the pond with soap. Let that be a lesson to you regarding the serious environmental values of local residents.

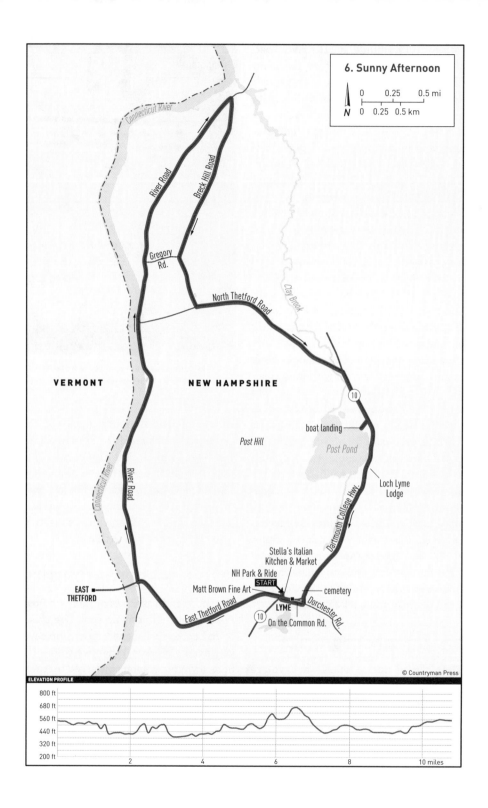

6. Sunny Afternoon

Connecticut River

River Road

Breck Hill Road

Gregory Rd.

North Thetford Road

Clay Brook

VERMONT

NEW HAMPSHIRE

Post Hill

10

boat landing

Post Pond

Loch Lyme Lodge

Connecticut River

River Road

Stella's Italian Kitchen & Market

NH Park & Ride

START

Matt Brown Fine Art

cemetery

EAST THETFORD

LYME

Dorchester Rd.

East Thetford Road

10

On the Common Rd.

© Countryman Press

ELEVATION PROFILE

800 ft					
680 ft					
560 ft					
440 ft					
320 ft					
200 ft	2	4	6	8	10 miles

AT A GLANCE Sunny Afternoon: Lyme

DISTANCE: 10.8 miles
ELEVATION GAIN: 756 feet
MODERATE

0.0   Start at the NH Park and Ride at the east end of the Lyme Town Common. Head west on East Thetford Road.

1.4   Turn right on River Road, just before the Connecticut River bridge.

5.5   Turn sharply right to start the climb up Breck Hill Road.

6.8   Bear left at the junction with Gregory Road, staying on Breck Hill Road.

7.2   Turn left onto North Thetford Road.

8.5   Turn right onto Route 10/Dartmouth College Highway.

9.0   Detour right to check out swim option at the Post Pond boat landing.

10.5   Diverge left, past church, cross Dorchester Road and take a right on On the Common Road.

10.8   Arrive back at the NH Park and Ride.

7

Over the Rivers and Through the Woods

Walpole, River Road, and Drewsville, New Hampshire; and Bellows Falls, Vermont

DISTANCE: 25.9 miles
ELEVATION GAIN: 1828 feet
CHALLENGING

One long or two shorter loops. The southern loop is like a trip to Kansas. The northern loop includes a wonderful stretch along the sparkly green Cold River and a visit to retro Bellows Falls. Together, they provide a remarkable diversity of Vermont and New Hampshire landscapes.

Walpole is far from being a lost village. Au contraire, it's one of those surprisingly grand, architecturally intact, monuments to northern New England industriousness. The many white, Greek Revival buildings (columns abound) are all impeccably restored, there's a spacious town green, nothing is out of place. There have been a variety of economic

engines over the years, but now this is the town that Ken Burns, of public television fame, has helped to revitalize. It's also the home of one of the finest restaurants in New Hampshire, so it requires a couple of rides, or one long ride linked by the village in the middle.

Park somewhere downtown behind Burdick's, the Walpole Grocery, and the Post Office. Lots of options here. Start out south along Main Street, and at the junction, head uphill to the right on what is at first Wentworth Road and then take a quick right on Old Keene Road for a mellow climb past small manses. The views to the west down to the Connecticut River and the Vermont hills keep you pleasantly occupied. Level out and then descend into the valley of Great Brook. Your first glimpse of expansive corn appears. At the bottom of this hill, just after the junction with Mill Road, note a pull-off on the left side where you can park later for a cool dip. It's another mile on Old Keene Road to take a left on Route 12.

After a quarter-mile, hang a right onto Halls Crossing Road and then a quick left on Bookseller Road. This used to be the main road that got left behind with the upgrade of Route 12. You should be able to figure out the building that housed the old bookstore. A mile of quietude brings you back to the traffic of Route 12. Unpleasant, but there's a wide shoulder for about 1.5 miles.

Just beyond the Amish furniture store (pricey, but quietly refined), take a sharp right onto River Road. Now the geospatial dislocation begins. There's a wonderful swoopy downhill away from trafficland. *Toto, don't you have the feeling that we're not in New Hampshire anymore?* It feels like you've been teleported to Kansas. The riverine floodplain soils along the Connecticut River provide some of the best farmland in New Hampshire. While farming has disappeared from many places in New Hampshire, it still holds on here. Flat cornfields, big herds of cows, and spring-flooded fields for migratory waterfowl, still dominate. After about 3 miles, pass Boggy Meadow Farm, makers of a delicious Baby Swiss that you can buy at the store in town. After a cathedral-like tunnel through massive oaks and more meadow expanses, you'll rise up onto Route 12 again.

Turn left, but only for a bit, and hitch right over onto North River Road, another discarded section of Route 12. At South Street turn right to go uphill back into the village. At the turn at the top of the hill, head straight ahead onto the One Way/Do Not Enter street, so you can cruise through a pretty neighborhood and around the town green. It feels like a set for *The Music Man*, gazebo and all. End the ride here, or perhaps catch a cold drink at the Walpole Grocery and continue for the longer, more challenging second loop.

Head north on the aptly named Old North Main Street. At the three-way junction with North Road and Old Drewsville Road, take the middle fork on Old Drewsville Road. This is the beginning of a long climb. Turkeys scuttle into the meadows, swallows dip, horses graze. Soon you're into the woods, climbing up Cheney Hill. This long climb pays off in a similarly long, swoopy, and curvy downhill on a newly paved road back into farm country where you'll cross Blanchard Brook and come to the crossroads with the Walpole Valley Road. Head straight ahead, continuing on Old Drewsville Road, passing a small private airstrip on your left, and

A SHORT DETOUR TO KANSAS ALONG RIVER ROAD

then after a mile turn right on Route 123 for the short jog into Drewsville. (Say you went to Drewsville to any of your friends who have lived in Keene for decades and they'll say, "Drewsville, where's that?" This gives Drewsville lost village cred.)

You might be tempted to think that Drewsville is defined by the country store at the crossroads, but be sure to take a spin around the classic, forgotten green that illustrates that at some point Drewsville was less lost and more prosperous. There's a grand old Victorian sprawl at the head of the green that was once an elegant hotel or stately home that's now a Headstart center.

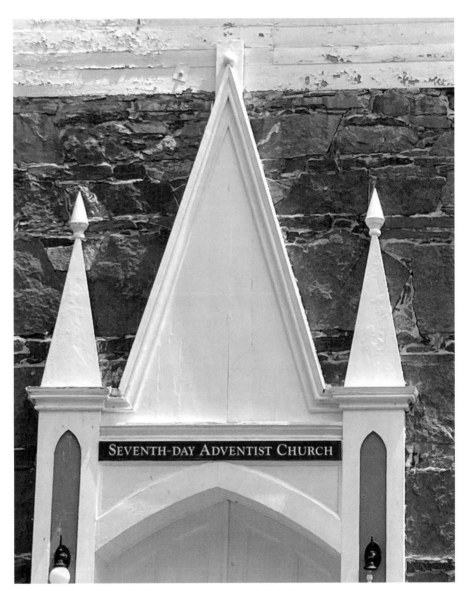

TREASURE HUNT: FIND THIS ARCHITECTURAL DETAIL ON THE DREWSVILLE GREEN

ONE OF MANY SWIMMING HOLES ALONG THE COLD RIVER

Head downhill steeply from the General Store, going north on Route 123 to cross the Cold River. Take a left on Cold River Road (ignoring the Road Ends or Dead End signs because it's perfectly bikeable past where it's closed to cars).

Now here's the real crème de la crème part of this ride. At first the gravel road is above the river, but you'll see a number of pull-offs with paths descending steeply through hemlocks down to Drewsville Gorge and numerous deep swimming holes. (Most with No Trespassing signs.) The road gradually reaches river level and you coast downhill with the river gamboling on your left. At some point, the road is closed to traffic and continues as a single track on the abandoned road. You'll want this to last forever.

Right after you pass another gate onto drivable road, look for a pullover on the left side free of No Trespassing signs. Follow the meager trail that gets wider and ambles along for a while and you'll start to think about turning around. Don't. Keep going. To a wonderful, over-your-head deep swimming hole with a gravelly beach. Sometimes there's an auditory backdrop of the groaning of the gravel-processing machinery coming from the Cold River Materials pits around the corner and on the other side of the river. Refreshing all the same.

Back on River Road you'll pass more appealing, yet less private, swim spots. This whole stretch is about 3.5 miles of joyful, beautiful, untrafficked riding. At the junction with Route 123, turn right, and then right again on Route 12 toward Bellows Falls.

The shoulder is wide, and sometimes there's a nice tailwind from the south pushing you up toward the geological wonder of the Connecticut River gorge that defines the edge of Bellows Falls. As you approach Bellows Falls, note the expansive train yard huddled under the cliffs of Fall Mountain—old coal cars, plush broken-windowed Pullmans. It's a testimonial to the grand but fading railroad era of New England.

To get into Bellows Falls you've got

two choices—you can lift your bikes over the Jersey barricades across from the trainyard (at both ends of the bridge) and you're immediately downtown. Or you can continue on up Route 12 about a half-mile and take the bridge across to the upper part of the village. I prefer crossing the closed bridge.

Some notes about Bellows Falls. Bellows Falls is gamely trying to lift itself up by its bootstraps and rise above its lost small city status. Bellows Falls is every bit as interesting as Brattleboro to the south, but whereas Brattleboro has three interstate exits, Bellows Falls has none. The two exits that serve Bellows Falls are out 3 or 4 miles either north or south of town. The other problem is that bridge with the Jersey barricades. Why hasn't it been fixed? Well, the actual border between Vermont and New Hampshire is not the middle of the river but the west bank of the river. That means the Connecticut River is actually all in New Hampshire and therefore the bridges are all maintained by the New Hampshire Department of Transportation. And whereas the bridge used to have lots of commercial value to Bellows Falls, funneling traffic right downtown, the bridge has very little commercial value to the New Hampshire skinflints who don't want to pay to fix the bridge.

Nonetheless, Bellows Falls has a great opera house, a beautifully intact old railroad station, puzzling American Indian petroglyphs in the river gorge, an emergent restaurant scene, a great antique furniture store, and an evocative compact downtown. Forty years ago I enjoyed buying a pint of Boone's Farms Apple Wine, wrapping it in a brown paper bag,

TREASURE HUNT: A WELCOMING SIGN ON ROUTE 12 AS YOU APPROACH BELLOWS FALLS

and sipping it in funky alleyways, pretending to be Jack Kerouac in industrial Lowell. Lots to explore here.

Assuming you've crossed the old, closed bridge, just continue straight ahead and you're smack dab in the center of town. Nice coffee shop on your left and the wonderful Moon Dog cafe down a bit on your right. Worth poking around. Take a left on Westminster Street, then a quick right on Church and a left on School. Here you'll be treated to the faded late 19th-century Victorian architecture from the city's better days. You can buy a lot of house for not a lot of money back in these neighborhoods. Read Archer Meyer's *Bellows Falls* for a good picture of the challenges of rural, small city poverty.

Now for a series of quick right and lefts to climb the hill up out of town on back streets rather than on a busy road. Left on Atkinson, right on Burt, left on Pine, right on Williams Terrace, and left on Pleasant. Seem more complicated than necessary, but trust me, it's the way to do it. Now take a right on Route 121/ Saxtons River Road.

Two options. Travel about 0.75 miles, through the lost village of North Westminster, and take a left on Gage Street down to a right on Covered Bridge Road.

Detour: For the funkier, more arduous, and more scenic option—from the corner of Pleasant Street and Route 121, after about 0.25 miles, take a left (One Way signs) steeply downhill on narrow Forest Road. It feels more like a bike path than a road. You'll eventually get grand views of Twin Falls. This used to be a popular swimming hole, but too many local teens have drowned here and swimming is now discouraged. After a bit of climbing, you'll take a left on Covered Bridge Road.

Cross the river and start a long climb up a narrow, dark valley that feels far away so soon after urban Bellows Falls. The wilderness feel is dismissed at the top when you find yourself next to the zooming traffic of I-91.

Past Bald Hill Conservation area, Covered Bridge Road becomes Henwood Hill Road, and there's a pleasing downhill, out of the woods, across a marshy causeway to Route 5. Make a quick stop at Allen Brothers Farm Market for cider donuts. Then head south on Route 5 to the slightly lost village of Westminster Station. Not really lost because the convenience store/gas station right here is always hopping. Take a left on Route 123 and drop down and through the pinch of a road under the railroad tracks. (Many years ago, I came upon a semi that wasn't aware of the low clearance of this underpass and it was jammed between the tracks and the road.) You'll fit fine, and then you'll cross the Connecticut River Bridge back to New Hampshire. Right on Route 12 for about a mile, left on South Street. At the top of the little climb on South Street, go straight ahead on Elm Street (ignoring the One Way/Do Not Enter signs) to slip into Walpole the back way around the green. Home sweet home.

DINING OPPORTUNITIES

It's de rigueur to stop in at **Burdick's Restaurant and Chocolates**. If nothing else, stop for a hot chocolate, or a cold iced chocolate, or a few, irresistibly cute chocolate mice. The ambiance is country French and tres chic. The cuisine is refined, the interior softly lit and gracefully decorated. There's a copper-covered bar where Ken often lurks. The steak frites will transport you to Paris, the French onion soup is classic, and the lemon vinaigrette on the salmon is piquante. We like changing from sweaty bike gear into evening wear in the car to extend the geospatial dislocation experience from rural New England to Kansas farm country to cosmopolitan Paris in the wink of an eye.

A new arrival in the Walpole dining scene is the **Hungry Diner**, north on Route 12.

Great local beer selection, conscientious farm-to-table sourcing, an almost Vermont-like feel. More suitable for a post-ride quaff in your still-sweaty bike togs.

Moon Dog Cafe used to be our most favored post-ski lunch spot in Chester after skiing at Okemo on Wednesday mornings. I loved walking into what felt like a 1969 Vermont hippie museum. We were disappointed when they moved to Bellows Falls, but the food is still as creative, though the ambiance is more 21st century. Hearty soups, inventive salads, burgeoning sandwiches on artisan bread, and the most unusual plate garnishes ever.

SWIMMING OPPORTUNITIES

Great Brook. Head back to that swimming hole on Great Brook that you passed around mile 3. There's a small pull off just after the intersection of Mill Road and Old Keene Road on the left. Stroll down to the end of the guard rail on the right to find a slender footpath down to a small, pretty little swimming hole. Crystal clear water, a smooth gravelly bottom, dappled sun through the hemlocks, and you're not visible from the road. It's charming.

You biked by all of them along the **Cold River**. Hard to beat this array of options—the holes are evocatively green and the water always brisk. I gave you directions above for one good option, but there are numerous other choices, awaiting your adventurous spirit to find them. The Cold River is as good as it gets for swimming holes in this part of New Hampshire.

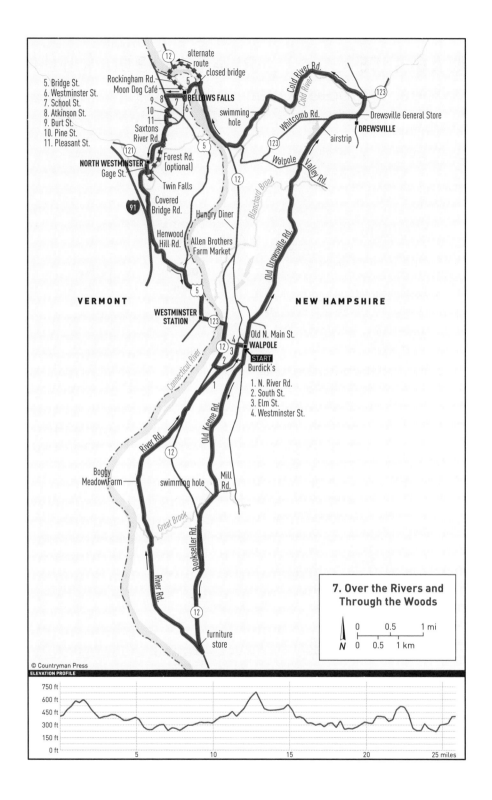

5. Bridge St.
6. Westminster St.
7. School St.
8. Atkinson St.
9. Burt St.
10. Pine St.
11. Pleasant St.

12 alternate route
closed bridge
Rockingham Rd.
Moon Dog Café
5
BELLOWS FALLS
9 8 7
10 6
11
Saxtons River Rd.
swimming hole
Cold River Rd.
Cold River
123
Whitcomb Rd.
Drewsville General Store
DREWSVILLE
123
airstrip
Walpole Valley Rd.
121
NORTH WESTMINSTER
Gage St.
Forest Rd. (optional)
5
Twin Falls
Covered Bridge Rd.
91
12
Hungry Diner
Blanchard Brook
Henwood Hill Rd.
Allen Brothers Farm Market
5
Old Drewsville Rd.

VERMONT
NEW HAMPSHIRE

WESTMINSTER STATION
123
123
12
Old N. Main St.
4
WALPOLE
3
2
START
Burdick's
1

Connecticut River

1. N. River Rd.
2. South St.
3. Elm St.
4. Westminster St.

Old Keene Rd.

River Rd.
12
Boggy Meadow Farm
swimming hole
Mill Rd.

Great Brook

Bookseller Rd.

River Rd.
12
furniture store

© Countryman Press

7. Over the Rivers and Through the Woods

0   0.5   1 mi
N   0   0.5   1 km

ELEVATION PROFILE

750 ft
600 ft
450 ft
300 ft
150 ft
0 ft
          5   10   15   20   25 miles

AT A GLANCE Over the Rivers and Through the Woods: Walpole, River Road, and Drewsville, New Hampshire; and Bellows Falls, Vermont

DISTANCE: 25.9 miles
ELEVATION GAIN: 1828 feet
CHALLENGING

0.0 — Park in the lot behind Burdick's and the post office. Get out to Main Street and head south.

0.2 — At South Street juncture, head straight onto Wentworth Road/Old Keene Road and then right onto Old Keene Road.

2.3 — Pass junction with Mill Road. Good swimming hole on right.

2.8 — Left on Route 12.

3.0 — Right on Halls Crossing Road and then a quick left on Bookseller Road.

3.6 — Rejoin Route 12, take a right and head south.

4.9 — Just beyond the Amish furniture store, turn sharp right and downhill on River Road South. Welcome to Kansas.

6.8 — Bear left at Halls Crossing Road to stay on River Road South.

9.2 — Left on Route 12.

9.5 — Quick right/left onto River Road North.

10.0 — Right onto South Street uphill.

10.2 — Where South Street bends to the right go straight ahead onto Elm Street. That One Way sign doesn't apply to you.

10.6 — Back to where you started. End southern loop here or take a left on Old North Main Street to do the longer northern loop.

11.0 — At the three way intersection of Old North Main, North Street, and Old Drewsville Road take the middle option onto Old Drewsville.

13.6 — Continue straight ahead across Valley Road staying on Old Drewsville Road.

14.4 — Right on Route 123/Whitcomb Road.

14.9	Arrive Drewsville. Take a spin around the green. Continue north and downhill on Route 123 and cross Cold River.
15.2	Left on Cold River Road. Don't be concerned about Road Closed signs. At some point you transition onto single track and then back onto paved road.
18.0	Right on Whitcomb Road.
18.2	Right on Route 12.
19.3	Dismount, cross Jersey barriers, and cross closed Vilas Bridge. Continue on Bridge Street.
19.6	Arrive in center of Bellows Falls. Then turn left on Westminster Street.
19.7	Right on Church Street, left on School Street.
20.0	Left on Atkinson Street.
20.2	Right on Burt Street, left on Pine Street, right on Williams Terrace, left on Pleasant Street.

20.6	Right on Route 121/Saxtons River Road.
20.9	Optional route—left on Forest Road. Otherwise continue on Route 121.
21.4	Left on Gage Street.
21.5	Right on Covered Bridge Road. At top of the hill, the name changes to Henwood Hill Road.
23.4	Right on Route 5.
24.2	At Westminster Station Irving gas, take a left on Route 123, down and under railroad tracks and cross Connecticut River.
24.6	Turn right on Route 12.
25.2	Left on South Street. Do what you did before and . . .
25.9	Arrive back in center of Walpole Village.

8

Lost Villages Par Excellence

Lyndeborough Center and Davisville, New Hampshire

DISTANCE: 13.5 miles
ELEVATION GAIN: 1005 feet
CHALLENGING

A serene ride on lots of gravel roads with a bit of time travel back to the mid-19th century in the lost villages of Lyndeborough Center and Davisville. Not spectacular, but pleasantly pastoral and historic.

Start this ride in the village of South Lyndeborough, New Hampshire, on Route 31. Park either at the Lyndeborough Village Store or in the parking area for the church across the street.

Cross Route 31 and the still-active railroad tracks onto Putnam Hill Road heading east. When Putnam Hill Road heads uphill to the left, bear right onto Cemetery Road and stay on it for a while. Soon after leaving the village, you're on quiet, shaded gravel roads. After a mile or so you'll enter marshy meadows and the large sign for the Pinnacle Mountain Fish and Game Club. Lots of pursuable critters in these hills. At the junction with Brackett's Cross Road, bear left to stay on

Cemetery Road and start the climb up to the first time travel opportunity. At the juncture with Center Road, bear slightly left. The road is now paved, which makes this longish climb a bit easier.

At the top of the climb, step back into one of the purer lost villages in southern New Hampshire: Lyndeborough Center. Get off your bike and wander around the United Church and the Town Hall and the high stonewalled Town Pound. The pound is a fixture of many 18th- and 19th-century villages. When a pig or cow and sheep escaped its pen and wandered around town, neighbors would collect the animal and put it into the pound until its rightful owner came to claim it. There are great views of the Pack Monadnock Ridge to the west. I always appreciate the serenity of this off-the-beaten-path crossroads.

A Note on Lost Hilltop Villages: Lyndeborough Center is emblematic of one of the demographic trends that played itself out in many New England hilltown communities. The first town centers were often settled after the end of the Seven Years' War (also called the French and Indian Wars). They were located on hilltops because most of the early settlers were farmers. Farmers liked hilltops because they were less subject to frost than valleys and hollows and therefore often had longer growing seasons by about a month. Second, the elevated locations were breezier and therefore less buggy than lowland locations. And the prospect over the nearby valleys gave them a better view of nearby goings-on.

When water power and industry started in the mid-19th century, mills were located in valleys by streams. As people moved off farms and toward industrial sites, the village centers migrated downhill. Thus, we've got

THE LYNDEBOROUGH MEETING HOUSE CONSTITUTES THE CENTER OF THIS LOST VILLAGE

TREASURE HUNT: FIND THE TOWN POUND IN THE HILLTOP LOST VILLAGE OF LYNDEBOROUGH CENTER

Lyndeborough Center, the 18th-century village located up here, and South Lyndeborough, down in the Stony Brook valley. Many of the lost villages you'll pass through in this book are the result of this demographic pattern.

Leave the village heading west on Center Road. You'll start this long descent, passing meadows that were created during the sheep craze that dominated New England agriculture between about 1810 and 1840, when sheep outnumbered people in many towns. By the middle of the 19th century, 80% of New Hampshire land was deforested, and much of it was turned into pasture land for sheep. There's a nice mile-long downhill here before you start to climb again and eventually take a right on Winn Road. This quiet gravel road rises 200 feet in

elevation over a series of steps—short climb, bench, short climb, bench. After the top at the 205 mailbox, you start to head downhill. At the next intersection where Winn Road bears right, you bear left on Old Temple Road to drop back down to Route 31.

Go straight across Route 31 to drop even more and cross Stony Brook and the railroad tracks (note the abandoned stone arch bridge to your left) and then ramble along through quiet countryside. Just past Pettingill Hill on your left, take a left on Collins Road. There's no sign here, but you'll know you're on the right road in about 100 yards when you see the Not Maintained in Winter sign. I always seek out these roads. There are usually no utility lines so they're narrower and are often shrouded by a tunnel of shade trees, giving them an intimate feeling. They can also get a bit washed out if there's been recent heavy rain. At the next junction, take a left onto Burton Highway and enjoy a mostly pleasant 2% to 3% downhill grade for the next mile or so till you arrive in the lost village of Davisville.

At the Davisville crossroads, take a left on Frye's Mill Road to enjoy the detour to Frye's Measure Mill. If you catch it when it's open, definitely take the time to explore here. Going inside is like walking into an Eric Sloane book of 19th-century American handiwork and history. The Mill is listed on the National Register of Historic Places and has been water-powered since the 1850s. Some of the Mill's first products—including round and oval pantry boxes, measures,

and piggins—are still being produced on much of the original water-powered machinery. It's dimly lit and crowded, much of the water-powered machinery is intact (very cool shingle mill equipment), and you'll want to do all of your Christmas shopping right here. It's a unique place.

Back on your bike, continue east on Burton Highway, take a left on Isaac Frye Highway and then at the bottom take a left on Route 31. This is the draggy part of the ride. It's a mile-and-a-half slog up this busy state highway without much of a shoulder. Toward the top, get off Route 31 by taking a right on Glass Factory Road and a left on Cider Mill Road to enter the village in the old-time way. (Note that it was glass factories and cider mills that caused the demographic move from the hilltops to the valleys.)

A VIEW OF MEADOWS AND DISTANT HILLS FROM THE LOST VILLAGE OF LYNDEBOROUGH CENTER

SHAKER BOXES ARE ONE OF THE PRODUCTS OF FRYE'S MEASURE MILL

DINING OPPORTUNITY

It's a bit of a drive, but really worth it, to find your way to **The Hilltop Cafe** on the Temple Wilton Community Farm in nearby Wilton at 195 Isaac Frye Highway. Yes, it's the same road you were on for a bit, but there are lots of twists and turns needed to get there. Located on the grounds of a beautiful old farmhouse, it's mostly a breakfast and lunch place but is open for dinner as well on weekends. Extensive outdoor seating. The food is locally sourced, sustainably grown, really fresh. The menu is intriguing. Where else can you get . . . llapingachos, Peruvian stuffed potato pancakes? The Rustic Chicken and Biscuits is perfect comfort food. And you'll want to ask for the recipe for the Three Day Chocolate Chip Cookie.

SWIMMING OPPORTUNITIES

Right as you started up the final slog, you passed **Goss Park**, a Wilton recreational park with a nice swimming area with lanes, docks, diving boards, and a floating water slide. Five dollars admission for non-local residents. We haven't dipped here, but it looks quite inviting.

I've never tried this place, but it's often on the lists of great swimming holes in New Hampshire. One online guide says: *The beautiful falls and whirlpool at* **Old Wilton Reservoir** *makes it a popular swimming spot when the water is calm enough. From Route 101 in Wilton, follow the Isaac Frye Highway for about 1.5 miles. When you pass over a stream, look for a dirt road on the right. Park there and walk about a third of a mile to the falls!* If you make it here, send me an assessment.

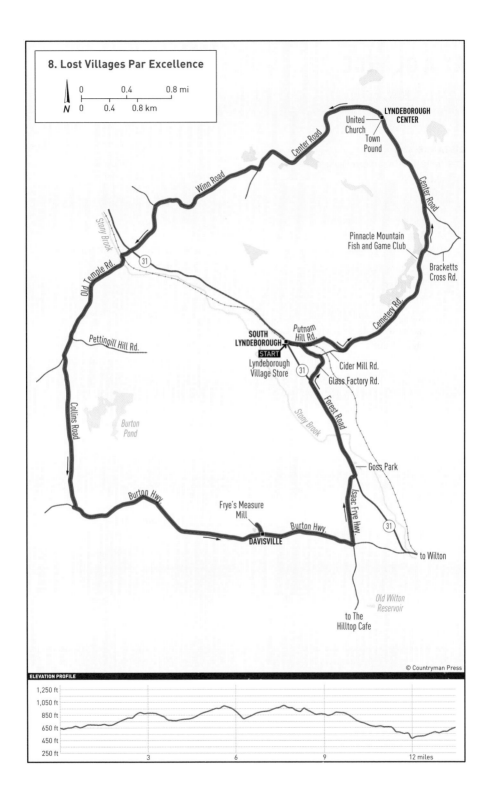

8. Lost Villages Par Excellence

0   0.4   0.8 mi
0   0.4   0.8 km
N

LYNDEBOROUGH CENTER

United Church

Town Pound

Center Road

Center Road

Winn Road

Stony Brook

Old Temple Rd.

31

Pinnacle Mountain Fish and Game Club

Bracketts Cross Rd.

Cemetery Rd.

Pettingill Hill Rd.

SOUTH LYNDEBOROUGH
START
Lyndeborough Village Store

Putnam Hill Rd.

31

Cider Mill Rd.

Glass Factory Rd.

Forest Road

Stony Brook

Collins Road

Burton Pond

Goss Park

Isaac Frye Hwy.

31

Burton Hwy.

Frye's Measure Mill

Burton Hwy.

DAVISVILLE

to Wilton

Old Wilton Reservoir

to The Hilltop Cafe

© Countryman Press

ELEVATION PROFILE

1,250 ft
1,050 ft
850 ft
650 ft
450 ft
250 ft

3   6   9   12 miles

AT A GLANCE Lost Villages Par Excellence: Lyndeborough Center and Davisville

DISTANCE: 13.5 miles
ELEVATION GAIN: 1005 feet
CHALLENGING

0.0 Park at the Lyndeborough Village Store in South Lyndeborough, NH, on Route 31. Cross the road and RR tracks going east on Putnam Hill Road.

0.4 Where Putnam Hill Road bears left and uphill, bear right on Cemetery Road.

1.8 At junction with Brackett's Corner Road, bear left to stay on Cemetery Road.

2.2 Bear left on Center Road.

3.0 Take a break to time travel in Lyndeborough Center. Continue west on Center Road.

4.5 Right on Winn Road.

5.7 Bear left on Old Temple Road.

6.2 Cross Route 31 and stay on Old Temple Road to descend and cross Stony Brook and RR tracks.

6.7 Stay left to stay on Old Temple Road.

7.4 Left on Collins Road. Not maintained in winter sign in about 100 yards.

8.7 Left on Burton Highway.

10.6 Take a left on Frye's Mill Road for detour back to the 19th century. After detour continue on Burton Highway.

11.4 Left on Isaac Frye Highway.

12.0 Left on Route 31.

12.9 Right on Glass Factory Road.

13.2 Left on Cider Mill Road.

13.5 Arrive back at Lyndeborough Village Store.

9

Railroad Heritage

Hancock, Elmwood Junction, and Eastview, New Hampshire

DISTANCE: 17.9 miles
ELEVATION GAIN: 1095 feet
MODERATE/CHALLENGING

A beautiful village, an evocative lost railroad world, extensive pond, river, and marsh views, and one of the prettiest back roads in the Monadnock Region. Pleasant isolation.

Start your ride in the classically beautiful village of Hancock. Park in the Norway Pond beach parking lot or to the left of the PO or across the street in the lot in front of the old school/now town offices. They're never crowded. Head east along Main Street through the core of the village. Wouldn't you like to live in this idyllic village, complete with a cafe, an inn with a pub, a general store, a lively library, and a sophisticated local music scene?

The beginning of this ride is a sleeper. Nothing spectacular, but every time I do the first half, I like it a little more. At the end of Main Street, bear left onto Route 137/Bennington Road heading north.

This road doesn't qualify as a back road, but it has a decent shoulder and the views across marshes and farms keep you engaged. There's a gentle downhill along Moose Brook and then a quick uphill to a right turn on Elmwood Road. Now the fun begins. Elmwood follows a gradually sloping, mostly meadowed ridge with stunning views out toward Crotched Mountain and the Wapack Range to the east.

At the juncture with Route 202, hang a right and then a quick left onto South Elmwood Road. Now, a historical detour. Take a left on Robinson Road and drift back in time to Elmwood Junction.

This was a busy place from the later part of the 19th century until the 1930s. Elmwood was the junction between the Manchester & Keene and the Peterborough & Hillsborough Railroads. There was a substantial station, coal sheds, coal loading tracks, water tanks, the station agent's house—a whole world unto itself. The massive floods of 1936 followed by the 1938 hurricane were the one-two punch that washed out many trestles and sections of track on both of these lines. Eventually this junction was bypassed in 1952, and very little remains of it. There's great interpretive signage and a short interpretive trail. Check out the washed-out bridge with pretty views across the wetlands. You'll be on a section of this same Peterborough to Hillsborough line in about 20 minutes.

Head back along Robinson Road and then continue straight, going south on South Elmwood Road. You'll drift down along the shores of Powder Mill Pond with even closer views of Crotched Mountain. Quiet and soothing. Once you reach Forest Road, take a right, and after 0.4 miles keep your eyes peeled for what looks like a driveway on your left—actually the beginning of the rail trail

THIS REMARKABLY USEFUL INTERPRETIVE PANEL WILL BRING ELMWOOD TO LIFE

you want to take. You'll know it's a rail trail because you'll see a similar straight section of abandoned railbed on the opposite side of the road. Take the left on this driveway and then bear slightly right onto the railbed in about 0.1 miles. This next stretch is dreamy. You're riding along the abandoned meanders and twisty course of the Contoocook River, passing marshes and meadows. There's a great stone culvert stop in the middle that could serve as a slightly spooky swim spot. The trail is sometimes root-laden but easily bikeable.

At Cavender Road, take another quick detour to the left to the old bridge, now for pedestrians and bikes only, over the Contoocook. It feels so swampy and southern that I'm always compelled to hum, *When Billie Joe MacCallister jumped off the Tallahatchie Bridge* here. Head back to the west, pass the rail trail, across Ferguson Brook, and continue on out to Route 202 through more meadows.

Cross 202 and take a left on Route 123 for just about a thousand feet.

(If you wish to make this a shorter ride, turn right on Route 123 and head back up into Hancock village in a couple of miles.)

When Route 123 bends to the left, continue straight ahead onto Tannery Hill Road. Yes, there's a climb up an 8% grade, but it doesn't last long. Go right on Middle Road past a couple of classic old homes and barns to Vatcher Road. Now there's a stairstep climb of three steps up around the corner to the bridge across an arm of Half Moon Pond.

Stop here to enjoy this remarkable bit of engineered landscape. You'll see that Half Moon Pond extends into a channel that is dammed and then continues east, bony and dry. In 1936, a flood on the Nubanusit Brook (we'll follow it in a few minutes) destroyed much of downtown Peterborough. To avoid a recurrence, Edward McDowell Dam was built to protect downtown Peterborough. In the event of a really big flood, the water backs up from McDowell Reservoir, and if the flood pond gets really high, it backs up through about 5 miles of marshes into Half Moon Pond. If it gets really, really high, Half Moon Pond overflows the dam underneath you and flows down that dry channel into Ferguson Brook and then into the Contoocook River, a few miles below Peterborough, thus saving downtown Peterborough from being flooded again. (We have The Army Corps of Engineers to thank for the preservation of these thousands of acres of wetlands and forests that provide excellent wildlife habitat.)

Jump back in the saddle, up a bit of a hill, and then turn right on Sargent Camp Road for a swoop down through Sargent Camp, a retreat center owned by Boston University. You'll skim the shore of Half

HEADING SOUTH ON THE RAIL TRAIL THROUGH MEADOWS AND MARSHES

TREASURE HUNT: ONE OF MANY ELEPHANT-SIZED GLACIAL ERRATICS ALONG THE OLD DUBLIN ROAD

Moon Pond, a possible swim spot, and roll along through pleasant woods, and past canoe-able preserved wetlands till you come to Route 137. It's another mile straight ahead to the lost hamlet of Eastview. Appreciate how that nice placid little stream on your left can turn into a raging torrent.

Eastview, in the eastern end of Harrisville, won't feel like much, but there was a mill and a railroad depot here once, where the Hancock Road crosses Nubanusit Brook. Without crossing the brook, we'll turn right on Jaquith Road for the choicest part of the ride back to Hancock. This is also the heartland of the Harris Center for Conservation Education's preserved land, so you'll pass lots of explorable places along the way.

Right away, you've got to climb on Jaquith Road, about 150 feet over the first half-mile. At the top of the first rise, you'll pass the railroad grade heading east and west. The railbed to the west is a great way to travel up to Harrisville through a bit of woodsy and marshy wilderness. Continue the climb and then there's a nice curvy downhill swoop and the meadows open out. Now the pastoral elegance begins. Each house is well preserved or handcrafted and the fields are beautifully maintained. After a bit of a steep climb, stop at Merrill Four Corners to appreciate the expanse of meadows. Just down the road heading south, there's a designer-perfect set of ice-skating ponds for a December outing. But for now, you're heading east along a lilting back road that alternates between woods stocked with mammoth glacial boulders and meadows strewn along a marshy stream. It's mostly downhill for the rest of the ride. I challenge you to find a road as appealing as this in the Monadnock Region. About a mile along here, pass the parking for the Cadot Trail to the summit of Mt. Skatutakee.

After another mile or so, you'll take a right and continue along Old Dublin Road. Classic Capes abound, and eventually there's a plunging downhill.

You'll probably miss the cool waterfall on your right as you zip past. Almost at the bottom of the hill, you've got to bear left for one last steep climb back up into Hancock Village. Norway Pond's water awaits you.

DINING OPPORTUNITY

Fiddleheads is a small cafe next to the Hancock Cash Market. Good seating options inside and outside. This is a great place for lunch. There's an array of fresh salads, good cupcakes and cookies, a couple of choices of burritos, and diverse sandwiches. Lots of the ingredients are sourced locally, and if you do this ride on a summer Saturday, you can track down these sources at the local farmers' market across the street behind The Hancock Inn.

SWIMMING OPPORTUNITY

Norway Pond is your classic village town beach. It's down behind that prominent Congregational Church in the center of town. There's a narrow beach, a rambly dock that encloses the little kids' swimming area, and a float further out to swim to. The water is tannin-stained but completely clean. Meadows tilt down to the water, the steeple of the church towers above you, and children laugh. It's an Edenic little scene.

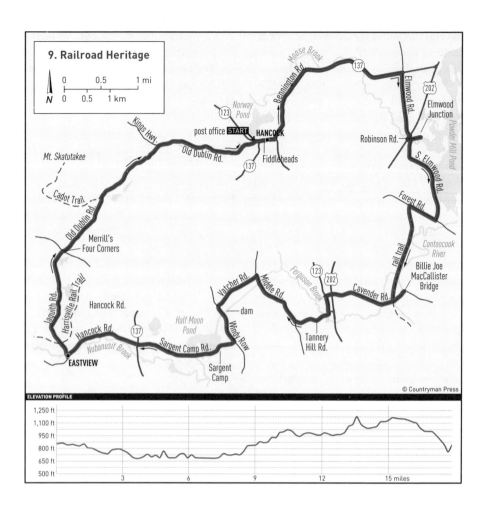

AT A GLANCE Railroad Heritage: Hancock, Elmwood Junction, and Eastview

DISTANCE: 17.9 miles
ELEVATION GAIN: 1095 feet
MODERATE/CHALLENGING

0.0 Park in the center of Hancock at the beach or town offices parking lots. Head east on Main Street.

0.3 Left on Route 137/Bennington Road.

2.7 Right on Elmwood Road.

3.6 Right on Route 202 and then a quick left on South Elmwood Road.

3.7 For detour to Elmwood Junction, left on Robinson Road. Return to South Elmwood Road and continue south.

4.9 Right on Forest Road.

5.3 Left on driveway that becomes railbed trail.

6.7 At Cavender Road take a detour to the left to enjoy the "Billie Joe MacCallister" bridge, and then return back to this spot. Continue west on Cavender Road.

7.5 Cross Route 202 to stay on Cavender Road and then left on Route 123. (Option to make this a shorter ride by turning right on Route 123 back to Hancock in a couple of miles.)

7.8 Where Route 123 bends to left, continue straight head onto Tannery Hill Road.

8.4 Right on Middle Road.

9.2 Left on Vatcher Road. When it bears left, it becomes Windy Row.

10.4 Turn right on Sargent Camp Road.

11.8 Cross Route 137 and continue straight ahead on what is now Hancock Road.

12.9 Arrive in the lost village of Eastview. Turn right on Jaquith Road.

14.4 Reach Merrill's Four Corners and stop for the view. Continue straight ahead on what is now Old Dublin Road.

16.4 Bear right at junction of King's Highway and Old Dublin Road to stay on Old Dublin Road.

17.5 Bear left to stay on Old Dublin Road and arrive at Hancock village.

10

Land of Lakes
Chesham, Nelson, Harrisville, and Dublin, New Hampshire

DISTANCE: 19.3 miles
ELEVATION GAIN: 1465 feet
CHALLENGING

A two-in-one ride. Choose either one longer ride or two shorter options. Three lost villages, ponds, and lakes abound. The heart of New England.

Drift into the village of Harrisville at dusk on a January evening. It's snowing lightly, flakes wafting down. Squint a bit so you don't see the utility lines and poles and ahhhh, you've slipped through the time portal back to the late 19th century. Weavers are tucked into their woodstove-warmed homes, the mill is just finishing up burning its one cord of wood on this frigid day when it never got much above 10° F. Harrisville is a National Historic Landmark and one of the most architecturally intact small brick mill villages you'll find anywhere in New England. It's easy to feel long ago and far away here. The same is true of the village of Nelson—it feels like a frozen-in-time Currier and Ives print.

Most likely you won't be biking in midwinter, but you'll still get the lost village feeling arriving in Nelson and Harrisville in the other three seasons. On the continuum of 1-10, 1 being completely found, like downtown Manchester (VT or NH), to 10 being *Brigadoon*-ish lost, Harrisville is about a 7, pleasantly lost, remarkably preserved. Nelson is about an 8—it doesn't have businesses in the village the way Harrisville does. You rarely pass through these places on the way to anywhere else. Don't miss the epicenter of craft weaving in North America at Harrisville Designs or the culinary delights of the Harrisville General Store. And, if you can arrange to be in Nelson on a summer Monday night, be sure to attend the contradance, a well-preserved tradition in the lost New Hampshire hills.

It's best to arrive in Nelson and Harrisville on bike, letting the villagescapes unfold slowly, at a horse-drawn carriage pace. So you'll start in Chesham, one of the villages of the town of Harrisville. Park at the Wells Memorial School in Chesham or across from the church in a wide gravel lot. Head north on Chesham Road for a quick downhill. At the nicely preserved Chesham Depot, bear right and east along the shores of Chesham Pond toward Harrisville. At the outlet for the pond dam, there's a new interpretive panel that provides a rich history of the area.

In brief, it's interesting to understand all these ponds and reservoirs you're passing by. In the late 1920s and early 1930s, rural electrification came to southwestern New Hampshire. To provide hydropower, many of the lakes and ponds in Harrisville, which sits up high on the watershed boundary between the Merrimack and Connecticut Rivers, were dammed to provide a constant flow of water to a hydroelectric station in Marlborough. Silver Lake, Child's Bog, Chesham Pond, Seaver Pond, Russell

ONE OF MANY MONADNOCK VIEWS—THIS ONE ACROSS CHILD'S BOG

Reservoir, and Howe Reservoir were all dammed, or had the dams raised, as part of this rural electrification. It was like a miniature TVA project. And it's why there are so many wildlife-rich and swimmable bodies of water on the western, Chesham end of Harrisville.

After Chesham Pond, you'll take a left on Seaver Road and gradually climb toward Silver Lake. *(For the shorter Harrisville Dublin loop, continue straight here and rejoin directions at 9.3 miles in At a Glance on page 89.)* You'll cross the dam at Seaver Pond (no houses, good swim spot) and then climb through the meadows of the old Seaver Farm. Make sure you turn around to take in the mondo view of Monadnock across cleared fields when you get to the remaining barn. Hitch left to come out on the paved road at the Silver Lake outlet.

Silver Lake Land protection: Silver Lake is one of the choice lakes in southern New Hampshire (along with Nubanusit and Dublin Lake in these parts). All of them are spring-fed, deep, and crystal clear. Edgar Seaver owned this farm and much of the land on both sides of Silver Lake. When Edgar died, the property around Silver Lake had already become a premier summer cottage destination for banana belt Keene residents, where it's always 5–10 degrees hotter in the dog days of summer. Local conservationists were concerned that more summer houses would sprout up on all this lakeshore property, and so land protection began in earnest. The meadows of this farm (worth millions on the open market) and much of Edgar's land have since been put into conservation easements through the hard work of the Harris Center and the Silver Lake Land Trust. Because of their efforts, we can all appreciate the still pristine water quality of Silver Lake.

Turn right on Breed Road (so-named on the maps—around here we just call it the Silver Lake Road) and climb past an orange house and then descend to the shore of Child's Bog. This was a bog before it was logged and dammed as part of the rural electrification project mentioned earlier. At the end of Child's Bog, look right for another grand Monadnock view.

At the Nelson Road, turn left. After about 1.25 miles, pass Hardy Hill Road and continue straight ahead past a swamp and then an expansive view across marshlands. You'll climb a bit, bend around a corner, and then Brigadoon—the Nelson town green, the stately church, the tiny old library and the new one connected to the town hall. It's lovely in its simplicity. Sit on the bench and take it in. Imagine the town hall alive with fiddle music, rhythmic floor stomping, twirling couples, group gaiety. In sociological terms it's called *collective effervescence*—the sense of communion or fusion that occurs when a group of people are enjoying themselves together. You'll feel it if you return here for a dance.

Back in the saddle, it's a short steep climb uphill to the village cemetery. Turn in here. This scene evokes the third act of *Our Town*, looking down on the village from the cemetery. Completely serene. Past the cemetery, take the left hand fork on Hardy Hill Road and slide back down to the Nelson Road heading south. It's another nice downhill drift on pavement back to the Child's Bog corner.

THE BRICK VILLAGE OF HARRISVILLE—A NATIONAL HISTORIC LANDMARK

Continue straight on the Nelson Road along the north shore of Child's Bog, climb a bit, and then descend to the shores of Harrisville Pond. (Count them—this is the fifth pond or lake you've passed in the last 8 miles.). The village appears ahead of you across the pond. At the juncture with Chesham Road (big yellow house on the corner, slightly out of place—long story), bear left. *(For a shorter loop excluding Dublin, turn right here and head back to the car.)*

Note the seemingly floating public library on your left, and the brick mill buildings now revitalized and housing diverse small businesses. Harrisville Designs, in the center of the village, is the epicenter of the craft weaving world in the United States. Make a quick stop at the Harrisville General Store for iced coffee or to decide whether to come back here for a post-ride lunch or snack.

From the store head east out of town, a quick plummet past the mill complex, paralleling Nubanusit Brook. Skip the two left-hand turns down both sides of Skatutakee Lake and the right turn to the dump and start the long, slow (2 miles, 250 feet) climb up the Dublin Road.

This section is only mildly scenic, but it's a reasonably pleasant slog. Sometimes we save stories or new jokes to keep us occupied on this climb. Or try this—are prime numbers evenly distributed in each 10-number span (i.e., 1–10, 11–20, 21–30, and so on) up to 100? Math puzzles like this are good for long climbs. Once you get to the absolute top of this climb, at the 35 mph sign, the views to the east get better. The Wapack Range stretches from Temple Mountain up to South and North Pack Monadnock.

Meanwhile, you'll pass the Dublin School's Nordic ski network on your right and you can look for signs of one of New Hampshire's lost downhill ski areas in

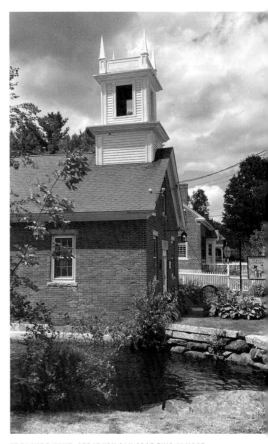

TREASURE HUNT: SEE IF YOU CAN SPOT THIS ALMOST-AFLOAT, TINY PUBLIC LIBRARY

this stretch. After you pass the Dublin School campus, turn right and then right again on Old Common Road for a short steep climb. At the top, bear left on Frothingham Road to intersect Route 101.

Detour: *For a scenic detour, at the top of this hill, bear right staying on Old Common Road, pass Old Pound Lane, and a bit further along, take a left on a lane through the cemetery with great views west across Dublin Lake toward Monadnock. Pause here and find the gravestones that illustrate the tragedy of Jacob and Martha, who had four infants perish at an early age.*

Cross Route 101 to get onto Lake Road. Now it's gravy for most of the rest of the ride. Amble around the lake, enjoying the manses of the golden era of the late 19th century. Mark Twain, William James, Abbott Thayer, and Rockwell Kent all rusticated here, enjoying the sparkly water and the paintable landscapes. Dublin, New Hampshire, whose town center you've just skirted because it's not a lost village, is the highest town center in New England at about 1400 ft., so enjoy the rarefied mountain air. Take a right at the end of Dublin Pond and pass the public boat landing. Lots of good places to slip into the pristine waters along here, should you be so moved. Lake Road dead ends into Route 101, and here you have to face the music: real traffic. But you're only on 101 for about a half-mile, and it's a great downhill cascade.

Swoop past the Friendly Farm (pettable lamps, chicks, goats) and look for a cluster of white buildings (Worcester's Antique Autos) on your right that landmark the turn. Dive down the rabbit hole as you turn right off of 101 onto Macveagh Road—fun to carry speed for the next little uphill, but be ready for the change from asphalt to sometimes loose gravel. There's a beautiful, recently reclaimed meadow, with a cordwood operation at the far end, and then you cross the town line from Dublin back into Harrisville. The next 1.5 miles provide one of our favorite stretches of backroads biking in the Monadnock Region. After Hill Number 4 (which heads uphill to your right), you enter an elegant, downhill hemlock tunnel that goes on and on. In the right autumn light, with sun dappling through the dense hemlocks, there's a psychedelic strobe effect. This languorous descent, mildly otherworldly, pops you out into shockingly green meadows on the right and a redwing blackbird marsh on the left.

At the four corners at Macveagh and Brown Roads, take a left on the Brown Road. It's deep woodsy until one last hill up to the old village center of Pottersville (so lost you won't recognize it as an old village center) with a mixture of old Capes (see if you can figure out which one the author lives in), new houses, and lots of meadows. Then it's a satisfying plummet downhill back to Wells Memorial School and the church.

DINING OPPORTUNITIES

The Harrisville General Store is a destination lunch spot. You'll find a great range of scrumptious breakfast sandwiches with locally sourced everything named after all the nearby lost villages. I recommend the Harrisville with Jodi Farwell's sausage. Make sure you ask for a side of green salsa. The cheeseburger on ciabatta is similarly delish. There are a couple of hand-crafted soups per day, to-die-for desserts, a great Mediterranean tuna salad, and beautiful sandwiches. You can sit on the porch overlooking the astutely restored and repurposed mill buildings. Notice that you don't notice cigarettes or lottery tickets for sale.

Even if you're not hungry, don't skip the store. There's a rebirth of the general store across northern New England, blending old-time community hub (drop in for beer, milk, and bread) with urban culinary refinement. Check out other rides in this book that take advantage of the Guilford Country Store in Guilford, Vermont, and the Petersham Market in Petersham, Massachusetts.

Dublin General Store. Everybody raves about the deli counter at the Dub Gen, giant $1.50 chocolate chip cookies and an interesting sandwich menu and good take out. My son swears by the curried chicken salad wrap. It's owned

NO UTILITY LINES ALONG MACVEAGH ROAD MEAN YOU RIDE THROUGH A COZY HEMLOCK AND MAPLE TUNNEL

by Andy and Michelle, and she always has different hair—check out the current style. But the Harrisville General Store versus the Dublin General Store is like the Red Sox versus the Yankees, and I'm a Harrisville resident, so you know my preference. But really, they're both great.

SWIMMING OPPORTUNITIES

If you're up for a swim, find your way to **Sunset Beach** on the backside of **Harrisville Pond** past Peanut Row. Walk. It's only a quarter-mile from the store to this sandy, shallow, kid-friendly beach. And come late in the day to enjoy the reason for the name. New Hampshire town beaches are one of the under-the-radar joys of living in them thar hills of the Granite State. (Sorry Vermont—you excel in many ways, but you just don't have the same plenitude of lakes and town beaches as New Hampshire.) Most town beaches are residents-and-guests-only,

but this is rarely enforced, and there are no beach sticker requirements. Most towns around here have so many summer residents that no one will be suspicious of your flatlander accent.

You passed **Silver Lake** early on your ride. It's our go-to swim spot on summer evenings. Something so refreshing about the crystalline green water. The downside is that on weekends, it has an active boat launch, so there's often the stink of outboards, and parking is at a premium. But, mid-week, at dusk, after a nice sweaty ride, you can almost have it to yourself. Find the stone steps at both ends of the parking lot and slip beneath the silvery surface. Loons might call. Your skin will feel like freshly laundered sheets after a swim here.

If Silver Lake is too crowded, park on the side of the road by the boat ramp on **Seaver Pond**. Or there's a parking area on the other side of the dam, and you can follow a bit of trail back to a rocky point. Both are fine swim spots.

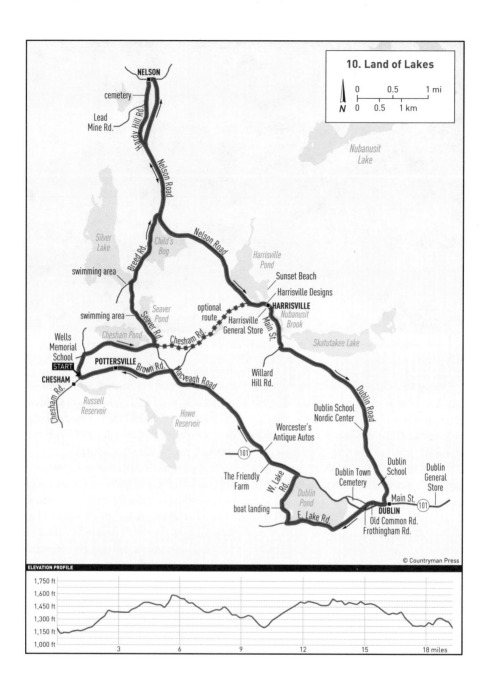

10. Land of Lakes

NELSON
cemetery
Lead Mine Rd.
Hardy Hill Rd.
Nelson Road
Nubanusit Lake
Silver Lake
Child's Bog
Breed Rd.
Nelson Road
Harrisville Pond
swimming area
Sunset Beach
Harrisville Designs
Seaver Pond
optional route
HARRISVILLE
swimming area
Harrisville General Store
Nubanusit Brook
Wells Memorial School
Chesham Pond
Seaver Rd.
Chesham Rd.
Skatutakee Lake
START
POTTERSVILLE
Brown Rd.
Main St.
CHESHAM
Chesham Rd.
Macveagh Road
Willard Hill Rd.
Russell Reservoir
Howe Reservoir
Worcester's Antique Autos
Dublin School Nordic Center
Dublin Road
101
Dublin Town Cemetery
Dublin School
Dublin General Store
The Friendly Farm
W. Lake Rd.
Dublin Pond
Main St.
101
boat landing
E. Lake Rd.
DUBLIN
Old Common Rd.
Frothingham Rd.

© Countryman Press

ELEVATION PROFILE

1,750 ft
1,600 ft
1,450 ft
1,300 ft
1,150 ft
1,000 ft

3   6   9   12   15   18 miles

AT A GLANCE Land of Lakes: Chesham, Nelson, Harrisville, and Dublin

DISTANCE: 19.3 miles
ELEVATION GAIN: 1465 feet
CHALLENGING

0.0	Park at Wells Memorial School or across from the church on Chesham Road. Start pedaling northeast and downhill on Chesham Road.
0.3	At Chesham Depot, bear right to stay on Chesham Road.
1.4	Turn left on Seaver Road. Turn left at top by lake outlet and . . .
2.4	Arrive at Silver Lake, turn right on Breed/Silver Lake Road.
3.4	At end of Child's Bog, turn left on Nelson Road. (Option to cut off the Nelson lollipop and turn right to go to Harrisville.)
5.4	Arrive at Nelson Village. Soak it in. Then head south, uphill on Hardy Hill Road.
5.8	Bear left at junction with Lead Mine Road to stay on Hardy Hill Road.
6.4	Bear right onto Nelson Road.
7.4	At Child's Bog junction, continue straight ahead on Nelson Road.
9.3	At junction with Chesham Road, continue straight ahead into village.
9.6	Mandatory stop at Harrisville General Store. (Option to cut off Dublin loop and head back to Chesham). After store, continue downhill on Main Street past turn-offs to Lake Skatutakee and Harrisville Depot.
10.3	At junction with Willard Hill Road bear left uphill on Dublin Road.
13.1	Turn right on Route 101.
13.2	Right on Old Common Road.
13.4	Left on Frothingham Road.
13.5	Cross Route 101 onto East Lake Road. Beautiful lake views.
14.7	Right on West Lake Road.
15.5	Left on Route 101. (Careful at this intersection.)
16.1	Right onto Macveagh Road.
17.9	Left on Brown Road.
19.3	Arrive back at Wells Memorial School and church.

An Escher Ride

Westmoreland and Spofford Lake, New Hampshire

DISTANCE: 11.5 miles
ELEVATION GAIN: 728 feet
MODERATE

A ride with a perfect elevation profile. Climb up through a serene lost valley, cruise a beautiful lakeshore, and finish with an endless downhill. This ride description first appeared in *The Keene Sentinel's* ELF magazine on 27 August 2020.

A ring of "hill towns" surrounds the old glacial lakebed of Keene. While Keene rides are mostly flat, the hill town rides tend to all have at least one moderate climb, and they're more scenic. Park at the Westmoreland Town Offices/Post Office complex in what's referred to as South Village in Westmoreland. Route 63 passes through so it rates only about a five on the lost villages scale, but it sure is pretty. If you're into jewel-box town libraries, check out Westmoreland's, just a couple hundred yards east on South Village Road.

Start your ride coasting slightly downhill south on Route 63 about 0.3 miles.

Just before crossing Partridge Brook, turn left, slightly uphill onto Spofford Road. After about a mile, you emerge into an elegant lost valley, sweeping meadows on both sides of the road, with the pointy little peak of Mt. Pistareen as your northern star. That's where you're headed. You'll cross a sparkly stream at 2.1 miles with a dip-able pool just on the right side of the road. If the moniker "Pleasant Valley" wasn't already claimed, it would apply here.

The meadows soothe, the quiet road lilts along, and then you start the climb. We like rides that start off easy, work into the major climb during the first third to half of the distance, and then level off and coast downhill in the later stages of the ride. This climb, up to Spofford Village, comes at exactly the right point in the ride. It's stepped, so you get a couple of breaks, the architecture is classic, and toward the top it narrows into a little

BEAUTIFUL MEADOWS AND BARNS ALONG SPOFFORD ROAD

THE BEAUTIFUL SHORELINE ROAD ALONG SPOFFORD LAKE

glen along the boundary of Chesterfield Gorge State Geological Wayside. The crux of this ride is the short, very steep pitch (15%+ grade!) into the village. Make sure to gear way down—it feels a bit like climbing a wall—but it's over quickly. Or, take the left at the base of the steep section to take a slightly less taxing route up to the South Shore Road.

Take a right onto South Shore Road/ Route 9A and amble through Spofford village, past a couple of abandoned stores and mills, into summer vacation land. Conveniently located halfway between Keene and Brattleboro, Spofford Lake is chock-a-block cottaged all the way around. Hardly an undeveloped lot. And though some of these summer homes have been glitzified and turned into year-round homes, many feel old-timey and cozy. Though not quite as pristine as Silver, Dublin, and Nubanusit Lakes to the east of Keene, this is also a spring-fed

lake, delightfully swimmable. You'll pass the public Ware's Grove Beach on your right—$3 for non-residents, shallow and family-friendly, and sometimes pretty crowded.

As the main road bears uphill to merge onto Route 9, continue straight ahead, through cottage-land till South Shore Road dead ends. An obvious bit of single track continues straight ahead and plops you out on Route 9 for about 500 feet. It's the right amount of time to make you happy you're not a road biker with the big semis barreling down on you. At the Route 63 intersection, take a right and leave much of the traffic behind. You're homeward bound. Saunter along the lake, the road clinging to the lakeshore.

A half-mile past the end of the lake, you're ready for dessert. Imperceptibly, the road starts to pitch slightly downhill, you accelerate, and you let go. The descent goes on and on and on. There's

The city of Keene deserves substantial credit for creating a very bikeable city. This includes converting both abandoned rail corridors (the Cheshire and Ashuelot Rail Trails), that crossed in Keene, into bike trails and building major bike/pedestrian bridges over two busy highways. Other cool bike trails have been developed as well, including the Jonathan Daniels Trail along the Ashuelot River and the Appel Way Trail connecting the hospital to Wheelock Park. Worth exploring. I really wanted to include a Keene-based ride in the book, but it didn't make the cut. More than enough options to keep you busy for a weekend.

a flat-ish spot in the middle, and then you keep going downhill. And just when you think it's all over, you go down some more, but it's never steep enough to require braking. Nothing monumentally scenic, mostly empty woods, a few houses, a few curves—all gravy.

This ride fits into our category of M.C. Escher rides. You've seen those Escher graphics that somehow trick the eye so that water looks like it's flowing downhill in a circle. You know it's physically impossible and you can't figure out how he manages to create the illusion. Similarly, there are bike loops that seem like there's way more downhill than uphill (which is impossible if you're biking a loop—they have to be the same). As the wind is whistling through your helmet along this stretch from Spofford Lake back to Westmoreland's South Village, you'll think, *Wow, this downhill goes on forever. Did we actually climb this much?*

At the bottom, you swoop out into meadows, pass your first turn, and yes there's a smidgeon of uphill back into the village. But you're so exhilarated that it's only a bit of a bother.

DINING OPPORTUNITIES

The old general store in the center of the village has recently been transformed into the **Barn and Thistle Eatery and Gift Shop**. It serves an array of breakfast options, scrumptious sandwiches and salads, and even afternoon tea. Completely cozy indoor seating and outdoors seating as well. This place makes this bike ride even more perfect.

If you want a raft of great dining choices, head back into Keene. On Emerald Street, tucked back from the street, is **Fire Dog Breads** (closes at 3 p.m.) Remarkably distinctive breads, great croissants, sandwiches on baguettes. I particularly like the Provencal (tuna, egg, bell pepper, marinated tomato, cucumber, olive, red onion). The Cuban is darn good as well.

Across the street is **Brewbakers**,

TREASURE HUNT: FIND THIS SIGN A BIT BACK FROM THE ROAD ALONG SPOFFORD ROAD

spacious indoor and outdoor seating. Hip salads (crispy artichoke), bowls (short rib hash), breakfast and lunch sandwiches (falafel pita). Freshly brewed, responsibly sourced, organic Terra Nova Coffee. Cheery place.

A few steps further, over on Main Street, is **Modestman Brewery**. Really distinctive and richly flavored beers and ales. If *The Most Beautifullest Thing in the World,* a double IPA, is on draft, be sure to at least taste it. Nice patio out back with heaters for cold season drinking and dining. The **Street Savory** food truck is there Wednesdays through Sundays. The smash burger with tater tots is sinful.

And, trust me on this. Go to **Athens Pizza**, order the chicken kabob plate with no fries, extra salad, and an extra pita. Healthy, inexpensive, feeds two people.

SWIMMING OPPORTUNITIES

To find **Partridge Brook**, head north out of the village on Route 63 and then take a left on Partridge Brook Road. This is the same pretty brook that you followed riding up Spofford Road. Right before the intersection of Partridge Brook Road and River Road, there's a pull off on the left and a tiny swimming hole within a Japanese woodcut landscape. Not very deep but completely refreshing.

If you're into more challenging swimming hole exploration, find your way to **Sheep Rock**, a hidden pool along another sparkly Westmoreland stream. From South Village, drive north on Route 63 past Partridge Brook Road up through the lost village of Park Hill. Down the other side, you'll cross a stream where there's space to pull over on the side of the road. Find the foot-trodden path through the meadow that then enters the woods going west along the stream. After a bit you'll see where the stream creates a little notch through the bedrock and spills into a shaded, crystal clear pool. Also delightfully refreshing.

And, of course, there's **Ware's Grove** on Spofford Lake. You passed it earlier. Small admission price, concessions, crowded with little kids, shallow and sandy, but still a suitable place to cool off after a summer ride.

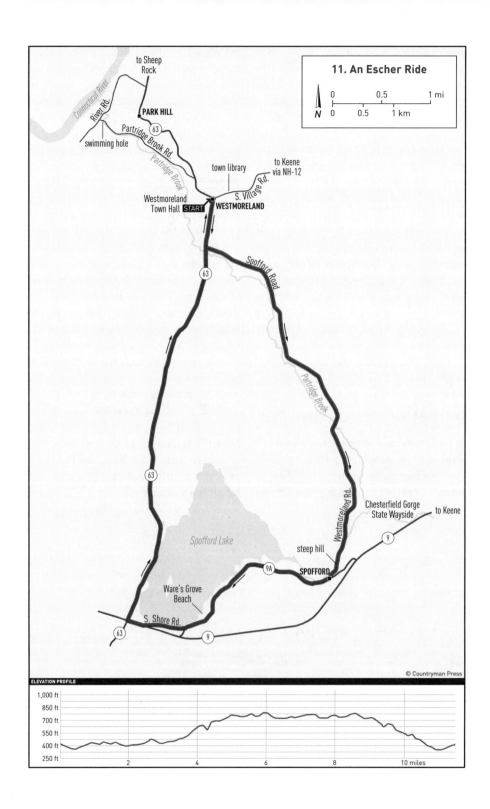

11. An Escher Ride

PARK HILL
to Sheep Rock
Connecticut River
River Rd.
Partridge Brook Rd.
63
swimming hole
Partridge Brook
town library
to Keene via NH-12
S. Village Rd.
Westmoreland Town Hall START WESTMORELAND
Spofford Road
63
Partridge Brook
63
Spofford Lake
Westmoreland Rd.
Chesterfield Gorge State Wayside
to Keene
9
steep hill
Ware's Grove Beach
9A
SPOFFORD
63
S. Shore Rd.
9

© Countryman Press

ELEVATION PROFILE

1,000 ft
850 ft
700 ft
550 ft
400 ft
250 ft

2   4   6   8   10 miles

AT A GLANCE An Escher Ride: Westmoreland and Spofford Lake

DISTANCE: 11.5 miles
ELEVATION GAIN: 728 feet
MODERATE

0.0 — Start at Westmoreland Town Hall. Head south on Route 63.

0.5 — Turn left on Spofford Road, which will turn into Westmoreland Road once you cross the town line. Steep 200-foot climb right before Spofford Village.

4.6 — Turn right onto South Shore Road through Spofford Village.

6.5 — Continue straight on South Shore Road. Do not turn left uphill at Prospect Hill Road.

6.9 — Continue straight ahead at dead end—obvious single track onto Route 9.

7.1 — Turn right and head south on Route 63. Now it's a straight shot back to the starting point with a great 2.5-mile downhill after the lake.

11.5 — Arrive at Westmoreland Town Hall.

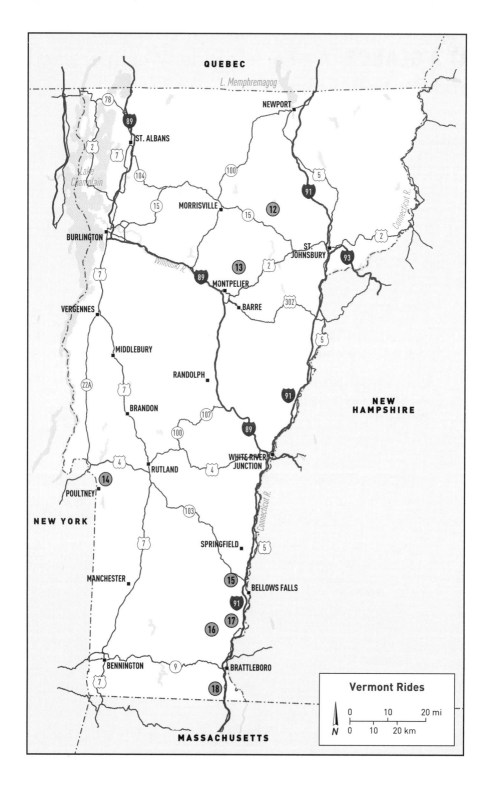

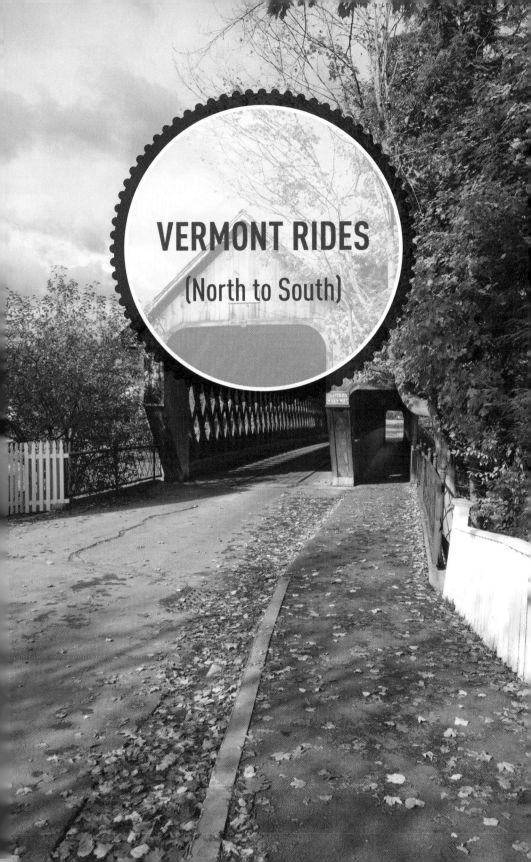

VERMONT RIDES

(North to South)

VIEW ACROSS CASPIAN LAKE FROM NORTH SHORE ROAD

If You Could Choose Only One

Greensboro and East Hardwick, Vermont

DISTANCE: 15 miles
ELEVATION GAIN: 1207 feet
CHALLENGING

This is, without a doubt, one of the prettier bike rides in Vermont. Endless, expansive, oh-my-god views across the Northeast Kingdom. And though there's lots of elevation gain, the grades are always manageable.

If you were to do an overnight trip to do only one of the rides in this book, do this one. Find your way to Greensboro on the shores of Caspian Lake. Not a lost village but a particularly appealing little village center with Willey's, one of the great general stores in Vermont. Stay at the Highland Lodge and do this ride, or one of the many other great rides in this area. To start this one, park at the little municipal lot across the street from the store. Or if that's crowded, park up the Craftsbury Road at the United Church of Christ.

Most of northern New England is forested. Vermont is 76% forested and New Hampshire is 81%. This means that a lot of the time, you're biking through mosquito- and deerfly-infested woods. But this part of the Northeast Kingdom is about 50% forested, with the balance being rolling, high elevation farmland. Rolling farmland makes for superb biking. When we finished this bike ride recently, my wife said, "Hands down. Most beautiful bike ride of the summer."

From the village parking lot head north on Craftsbury Road. Rise and fall as you head north. If you're observant you might see trail signs for the winter Nordic trails that are part of the Craftsbury Outdoor Center network that sprawls across Craftsbury and Greensboro. (We also went on one of the most beautiful Nordic ski loops here in the winter, on Barr Hill up to the right.) If you're a Wallace Stegner fan, his wonderful novel *Crossing to Safety* is set in this neighborhood along the shores of Caspian Lake. Soon after you pass the Highland Lodge, take a left on North Shore Road.

The next 8 miles are picturesque dirt/gravel roads. As you skirt the north shore of Caspian Lake, you'll see enticing driveways and grassy lanes leading down to lakeside homes and cottages. Caspian Lake is a glacial, freshwater lake, strikingly clear and well-protected. The views down through well-maintained meadows will make your mouth water. At Campbell's Corner, continue straight ahead on Lakeview Road/Town Highway 47. It's a long, straight climb through meadows. Toward the top, before you enter the woods, turn around to see the namesake view. After you top out near Harrington Road, there's a delicious downhill to a left on Overlook Road.

Now for the piece de resistance of the ride. These next 4 miles are some of the best backroads biking in Vermont. The road rides the crest of a ridge between the valleys of Alder and

can be an ecstatic experience or one long dusty slog.

At about 8.5 miles, take a left on Renaud Road and plunge down into the valley of Porter Brook. You'll pass through the lost village of Hardwick Center, so lost it's pretty much invisible. Then cross the main road between Hardwick and Greensboro onto Hardwick Farms Road through the meadows of a vast dairy farm. The road becomes Brickhouse Road, and at the bottom of a steep descent you come to a bridge and the rather large, lost village of East Hardwick, a "side hill village spilling from the level of a plateau down a sharp incline in the valley of the Lamoille River." If you can put on your brakes as you spill off the plateau, consider a stop at Summersweet Gardens for a full English Cream Tea, just on the outskirts of East Hardwick.

Just before crossing the Lamoille, turn left on Church Street which will soon become Hardwick Street, and accept that all good things must come to an end. After spilling down off that plateau, you must now climb back up to it. It starts out tamely, passes the Congregational Church, and then starts to ascend. There's cute Bailey Brook to keep you company as you climb, but honestly, it's just a boring slog. Not much to look at for the 300-foot push up to the junction with the Bayley Hazen Road. This road is a remnant of a military road, built during the Revolutionary War, that was originally intended to support the invasion of Quebec. You can find other remnants of the road from Peacham up to Hazen's Notch in Westfield.

At the Bayley Hazen junction, you now enter the lost village of Hardwick Street, a half dozen stately homes strung along the road, and since you're now back up on the plateau, the meadows have

Porter Brooks, and most of this ridge is made of meadows. First, you'll get stunning views to the east, then you'll crest a small rise and views to the west unfold. Once you're past the Cobb Schoolhouse, now a summer rental, there's a refreshing downhill with views to the south. It's one of those painfully beautiful places where you're not sure you can take another sumptuous view. One caveat—we've been working on this ridge for a couple of years. Once we labored up 450 arduous feet from Lake Eligo to arrive on Overlook Road to find that it had been graded an hour earlier. The road surface was three inches of soft sand and gravel—tedious to bike in. The next year, after about a mile of well-packed surface, we crossed the town line out of Greensboro and the Hardwick road crew had just graded the next section. Not again! The third time was a charm in summer 2021, when it was well-packed for the whole 4 miles. So, luck of the draw. It returned. From here you can climb gently up to the juncture at Tolman Corner or, at 13.2 miles, you can turn right and get in one more splash of backroads and another steep climb up Country Club Road. It's prettier but it's also the steepest climb of the whole ride. At the end of Country Club Road, turn right on Breezy Avenue and cavort down into Greensboro. Always nice to end a ride with a scenic downhill.

DINING OPPORTUNITIES

I'm a big fan of English Cream Teas, (scone, clotted cream, strawberry jam, pot of black tea), but we've never been passing the **Summersweet Gardens** in East Hardwick at the right time. I suspect it's worth checking out.

Willey's General Store in Greensboro is a wonder to behold. It's been owned by the Willey family for five generations and it has everything. It's a gas station, hardware store, department store, clothing boutique, grocery, and deli. If you can't find it here, it's not worth having. The deli offers straightforward Vermont general store offerings, but you can also find gourmet Jasper Hill Cheese, made locally, and a zillion other snackables. Nice shaded tables in the green across the street for a picnic.

If you are a beer aficionado, you must make the pilgrimage to **Hill Farmstead Brewery** on Hill Road, about 3.5 miles from downtown Greensboro. You drive along empty dirt roads, arrive at an old sprawly farm, then enter the taproom, and you feel like you're in Brooklyn. The beers have won many international competitions, and some consider the Edward to be the ultimate American pale ale. Browse their website to sample the provocative

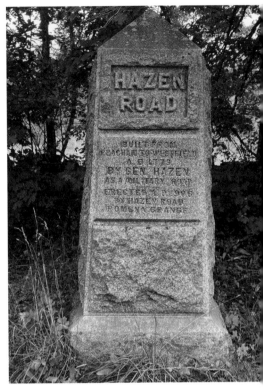

TREASURE HUNT: FIND THIS MEMORIAL STONE NEAR THE LOST HAMLET OF HARDWICK STREET

names of some of their other brews—Civil Disobedience, Fear and Trembling, Madness and Civilization, Self-Reliance. These brewers are both literate, and they make delicious, diverse beers.

SWIMMING OPPORTUNITIES

The obvious, easy to access, and pretty nice swim option is the **Caspian Lake Public Beach** located at the end of Beach Road, right opposite Willey's Store. Big parking lot, surprising big strand of sand for a Vermont lake beach, nice picnicking options. It can get kind of crowded here but the water is clear, the views are great and it's a hop, skip, and a jump from the end of your bike ride.

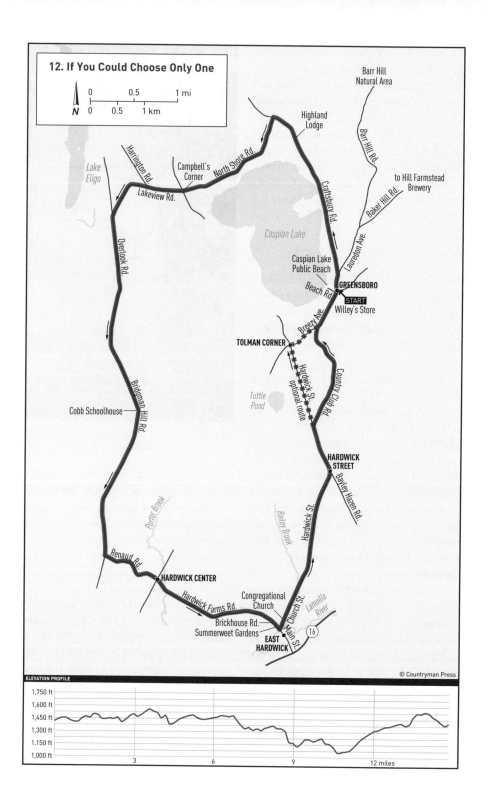

12. If You Could Choose Only One

Lake Eligo

Harrington Rd.

Campbell's Corner

North Shore Rd.

Highland Lodge

Lakeview Rd.

Barr Hill Natural Area

Barr Hill Rd.

Baker Hill Rd.

to Hill Farmstead Brewery

Craftsbury Rd.

Lauredon Ave.

Caspian Lake

Overlook Rd.

Caspian Lake Public Beach

GREENSBORO

Beach Rd.

START

Willey's Store

Breezy Ave.

TOLMAN CORNER

Country Club Rd.

Cobb Schoolhouse

Bridgman Hill Rd.

Tuttle Pond

Hardwick St. optional route

HARDWICK STREET

Bayley Hazen Rd.

Porter Brook

Hardwick St.

Bailey Brook

Renaud Rd.

HARDWICK CENTER

Hardwick Farms Rd.

Congregational Church

Church St.

Lamoille River

Brickhouse Rd.

Summerweet Gardens

Main St.

16

EAST HARDWICK

© Countryman Press

ELEVATION PROFILE

1,750 ft					
1,600 ft					
1,450 ft					
1,300 ft					
1,150 ft					
1,000 ft					

3   6   9   12 miles

AT A GLANCE If You Could Only Choose One: Greensboro and East Hardwick

DISTANCE: 15 miles
ELEVATION GAIN: 1207 feet
CHALLENGING

0.0 Park in the Greensboro town parking lot across the street from Willey's or at the church parking lot, a bit north of the village. Head north on Wilson Street.

0.2 Bear left on Craftsbury Road. (Right takes you toward Hill Farmstead Brewery).

2.1 Left on North Shore Road.

3.6 Continue straight onto Lakeview Road/Town Highway 47.

4.0 Bear left to stay on Lakeview Road.

4.6 Left on Overlook Road. After Cook Hill Road, this road becomes Bridgman Hill Road.

8.6 Left on Renaud Road.

9.3 Continue straight across Center Road onto Hardwick Farms Road.

10.9 Enter East Hardwick. Left on East Church Street, which soon becomes Hardwick Street.

12.8 Bear left to stay on Hardwick Street.

13.3 Right on Country Club Road. (Alternatively, just stay on Hardwick Street and then take a right on Breezy Avenue.)

14.6 Right on Breezy Avenue.

15.0 Arrive at Greensboro Village.

13

The Villages of Calais

Adamant, Maple Corner, and Kents Corner, Vermont

DISTANCE: 14.1 miles
ELEVATION GAIN: 1284 feet
CHALLENGING

This is an absolutely beautiful and classic back-roads Vermont ride. Also absolutely hilly. Mostly on dirt roads. Don't take on this ride unless you're really into embracing lots of short steep hills. But it's really worth it.

Find your way to Adamant, one of the six lost villages and hamlets within Calais, Vermont. Adamant was once known as Sodom because it didn't have a church. Villagers decided to change the name to Adamant to reflect the strength of the granite quarried in the area in the late 19th century. These villages of Calais appeal to me because most of them are at dirt crossroads; paved roads are pleasingly absent in this corner of northern Vermont. The dirt road access makes these villages feel more lost. Park at the Adamant Co-op, likely the smallest co-op grocery store in New England. I like Adamant because it hasn't

been fruff-ified—meaning it hasn't been gentrified or prettied up like Grafton or Woodstock. There is some beautiful stonework along the stream that flows from the upper to lower ponds, but mostly it feels like real Vermont. This ride will take you through two of the other lost villages of Calais—worth finding your way on winding, sometimes shockingly beautiful, back roads to all of them.

Park as out of the way as possible in front of the Co-op—limited parking—and then head west on Haggett Road. There's an initial climb and then you roll through forests and meadows. At County Road, turn right onto the only three miles of pavement on this loop. The landscape is beautiful but the hills are persistent. It's up and down and up and down and up and. . . . You'll find yourself thinking, really, another hill? Finally, you'll swoop

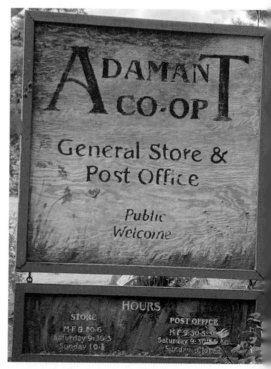

START YOUR RIDE AT ONE OF THE SMALLEST AND LOSTEST CO-OPS IN NEW ENGLAND

AN EPIC VIEW ACROSS MEADOWS TOWARD THE MOUNTAINS IN GROTON STATE PARK

down past the Maple Corner Community Store and Whammy Bar and back up to the dirt crossroads that define the largest of all the Calais villages. The community store is another co-op grocery, worth a stop, and there's also swim access to Curtis Pond in this village. More of those later.

From now on, it's all dirt/gravel roads. Continue north on what is now West County Road for another half-mile and then take a sharp right on Robinson Cemetery Road. For the next 4 miles it's lovely farm fields, shadowed lanes, and one beautifully preserved home or farm after another. It's an ode to the photography of the sadly departed *Vermont Life* magazine. As you descend into Kents Corner, note the sometimes open Kent Museum in the striking brick building at the corner. Then continue south on Old West Church

Road for more of the up and down and . . . you know the drill. Thankfully, after the junction with Lightning Ridge Road, the last mile or so along here is a continuous, effortless downhill to the shore of Sodom Pond (note that the village name changed, but not the pond name). You could easily just bear right here and be back at the Co-op, but you'd miss a completely different part of the ride.

Assuming you're up for it, turn left on Sodom Pond Road. After all those hills, this road follows the shore of the boggy pond and then the sinuous stream that drains the pond. It's blissfully flat and cozily closed in. But no good swim options here. After you cross the stream, the world opens up and there is an absolutely mondo view out across farm fields to the west and a grand old farm above you on the right. The view will take your breath away . . . which is too bad because you'll need it as you climb Sibley Road for another 250-foot elevation gain and then take a right on Center Road to face another hill or two as you descend to the Co-op. Beautiful all along here as long as you still have legs for hills. Make sure to stop in at the Co-op for a cold drink and a treat.

DINING OPPORTUNITIES

The **Adamant Co-op** is like a trip back in time to the 1970s. You must stop in. No deli options, but you'd be surprised how much can be packed into that small space. I also have a warm spot in my heart for Adamant because they sometimes host a black fly festival. My hometown in New Hampshire is rife with black flies and my softball team was the Black Flies. I like spunky Adamantians who know how to celebrate and revel in their adversities.

The **Maple Corner Community Store and Whammy Bar** is a new building (post-fire) so it doesn't have the same historic feel, but it's also a co-op and worthy of a stop. They do have a deli serving a hot roast beef on a toasted garlic baguette and good old PB & J. From their website: "Most unique is the Whammy Bar, a live music venue that hosts local and regional talent, as well as the famous open mic night. One night each week performers ranging from 10-year-old drummers to seasoned musicians take to the stage. All are greeted with respect and uproarious applause. The Whammy Bar typifies the soul and spirit of the community, where patrons and performers alike are embraced with unconditional positive regard." Each of these little Calais villages has its own distinctive identity and traditions.

TREASURE HUNT: FIND THIS MAUSOLEUM SOMEWHERE ALONG THE BACK ROADS BETWEEN MAPLE CORNER AND ADAMANT

SWIMMING OPPORTUNITIES

You passed the **Curtis Pond Swim Access** in the center of Maple Corner off to the left on Worcester Road. The swim access is a small dock on the shore with not much room to spread out. At one point, there were conversations about limiting access to just Calais residents, so check current guidelines.

Alternatively, wend your way through the maze of back roads in Calais to **Mirror Lake/No. 10 Pond** in North Calais. The boat access and beach are on the southern tip of the pond off of No. 10 Road with separate, adjacent parking areas. Park and walk 100 yards down to the beach. "Beach" is a generous term—it's more like a fine gravel strand no more than 30 yards long. But the water is crystal clear and there's a nice vibe. Perhaps walk a bit through the lost village of North Calais.

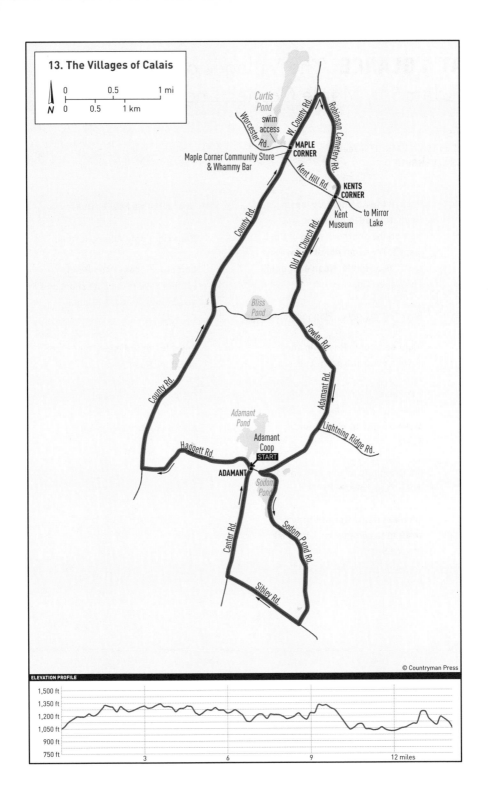

13. The Villages of Calais

N

0   0.5   1 mi
0   0.5   1 km

Curtis Pond

swim access

W. County Rd.

Robinson Cemetery Rd.

Worcester Rd.

MAPLE CORNER

Maple Corner Community Store & Whammy Bar

Kent Hill Rd

KENTS CORNER

Kent Museum

to Mirror Lake

County Rd.

Old W. Church Rd.

Bliss Pond

Fowler Rd.

County Rd.

Adamant Rd.

Lightning Ridge Rd.

Adamant Pond

Adamant Coop
START

Haggett Rd.

ADAMANT

Sodom Pond

Center Rd.

Sodom Pond Rd.

Sibley Rd.

© Countryman Press

ELEVATION PROFILE

1,500 ft
1,350 ft
1,200 ft
1,050 ft
900 ft
750 ft

3   6   9   12 miles

AT A GLANCE The Villages of Calais: Adamant, Maple Corner, and Kents Corner

DISTANCE: 14.1 miles
ELEVATION GAIN: 1284 feet
CHALLENGING

0.0   Park at the Adamant Co-op on Haggett Road in Adamant, a village on the southern edge of Calais, VT. Try to get out of the way as much as possible. Head east uphill on Haggett Road.

0.2   Bear left to stay on Haggett Road.

1.3   Right on County Road. Up and down and up and down and . . .

5.0   Pass Maple Corner Community Store and arrive Maple Corner. Stay straight on West County Road.

5.6   Sharp right to head south on Robinson Cemetery Road.

6.8   Arrive at Kents Corner. Stay straight to continue on Old West Church Road.

8.0   Bear left onto Fowler Road.

8.8   Bear right onto Adamant Road.

10.2   Left onto Sodom Pond Road. (Option here to cut ride short and go straight ahead to Adamant Co-op.)

12.1   Enjoy the grand view. Then right on Sibley Road.

12.9   Right on Center Road.

14.1   Arrive at Adamant Co-op.

Soft Rock Mining

East Poultney and Slate Quarries, Vermont

DISTANCE: 12 miles
ELEVATION GAIN: 948 feet
MODERATE

An unexpected ride in an untraveled corner of Vermont. Lonely lanes, an intriguing geological feature, and then an immersion in one of New England's rock quarrying industries.

A Note on Slate Valley Trails: I got intrigued with slate quarrying when my wife, then a 6th grade teacher, did a study of the slate quarries of Guilford, Vermont—in the southeast corner of the state. The slate industry flourished there in the mid-19th century and then moved to much more extensive slate beds in west central Vermont and the adjacent areas of New York around Poultney and Fair Haven, Vermont, and Granville, New York. Somewhere along the way, I stumbled across Slate Valley Trails, a volunteer community group building mountain bike trails and promoting gravel road loops in that area. The loop described here was inspired by the section on their website titled *Gravel Ride Network*. This loop has been thoughtfully designed to give you a taste of the diversity of this region. Use it as a stepping

stone to follow or create other backroads loops.

Though the Gravel Ride Network loops often start in Poultney, this ride starts in East Poultney, a slightly lost village with a beautiful town green, a charming general store, and a host of historical buildings. In fact, there are two museums: the Melodeon Factory and the East Poultney Schoolhouse, a Queen Anne architectural wonder. I like starting here because you get off well-traveled Route 140 sooner. Park by the General Store or somewhere around the green and then head east on Route 140.

Not much shoulder on Route 140, but

A QUARRY BOOM TOWERS HIGH ABOVE A SLATE "RUBBISH" PILE AND BIKER

you're only on it for a few minutes. The Poultney River is on your right, deeply cut down into the soft bedrock along here, so keep your eyes peeled for a pull-off on the right after about 0.4 miles for swimming hole access. Continue on Route 140 to a left on Finel Hollow Road. (For a slightly longer ride, continue on another mile to take a left on Hampshire Hollow Road—they both get you to the same point.) Finel Hollow starts out wooded, climbs steadily but not steeply, and then opens up into meadows. For the next 3 or 4 miles, you'll be on completely empty gravel roads—there's nary a car to be seen.

At about 3 miles, take a left on Watkins Hill and Pond Roads, and then

TREASURE HUNT: FIND THIS DECORATIVE QUEEN ANNE WINDOW SOMEWHERE AROUND THE EAST POULTNEY GREEN

another quick left on Watkins Hill. Now the fun begins. A big chunk of Watkins Hill Road is a "not maintained in winter" road, so it gradually narrows down to a shaded tunnel, with clover and grass in the mid-strip. There's a short steep climb and then you drop into a wondrous little cleft in the landscape along the upper stretches of Lewis Brook. Again, due to the same soft bedrock, this little stream carves a very steep-sided little gorge. In many places, the gorge falls away right next to the road. Stop along here to wander back to the cliff edge to find waterfalls and a mini-canyon. Very cool. You'll come out into abandoned meadows, pass some falling-down barns and beautiful houses, and feel like you're back of beyond.

Take a left at Gorhamtown Road to continue descending the Lewis Brook Valley, then a left on Lewis Road, and then a pretty quick right on Ward Road to arrive at Route 30. Quick right on Route 30 followed by an immediate left on Saltis Road. (Note here that you're crossing the rail trail that figures in a lot of the Slate Valley Trails rides.) On Saltis Road, you're back in classic farm country until you round a corner and—you're transported to the moon. Or at least a moon-like landscape of slate quarrying. There are expanses of vegetation-less hardscape, big piles of slate rubbish (the unuseful remnants of rock extraction), tall booms for rock-moving, and heavy equipment. It's otherworldly. And then, just as suddenly, you're back in farm country. Take a left on the York Street Extension and soon enough, you're back on the moon at a different quarry operation. Turn into the slate yard along here to look at slabs of slate prepared for transformation into roofing shingles, paving stones, and walls. After this second mine, take a left on Farnham Road and head back out to Route 30. Your moon trip is complete.

Just before getting to Route 30, you'll cross the rail trail. If you've had enough of back roads and hills, you can take a right on the rail trail, cruise down into Poultney, and then take Route 140 back to East Poultney. Completely flat. But here, I'll assume you're interested in backroads. Cross Route 30 onto Hannon Road for a quick but steep climb. Take a right on Lewis Road (you're back in the Lewis Brook Valley) and roll up and down until a final right on Hillside Road. Look for the informal museum of lawn sculptures on the left along here. The final half-mile is a gentle downhill coast back to the East Poultney Green.

DINING OPPORTUNITIES

It's important to support the revitalization of New England country stores, so stop in at the **East Poultney General Store**. It's small, but it has a nice little deli counter with salads and sandwiches. Really nice folks. We bought an excellent chicken pot pie here for dinner once we got home.

For a fuller dining experience, head back to **Taps Tavern** in Poultney. Excellent selection of craft brews, good pub menu. I always appreciate it when there's poutine on the menu. Young, smiley staff, and they have a local kickball team, so they know have to have fun.

SWIMMING OPPORTUNITIES

At the beginning of the ride, you passed that pullover on the right side of Route 140. Head back here and find the break in the guardrail. This provides access to a steep trail down to an outcropping above a fantastic little swimming hole in the **Poultney River**. Really deep,

ACTIVE FARMS ON FINEL HOLLOW ROAD

diveable-into, clear green water, completely refreshing. Down at the bottom of the hole on the right, there are little natural steps to get up and out of the pool.

This is the least crowded of the three swimming holes along here. There's another one about a half-mile farther along, and the third one is right before Route 140 crosses the river and the turn up Hampshire Hollow. Clear parking pullovers for each. We haven't tried these last two, so we would appreciate any assessments if you swim there.

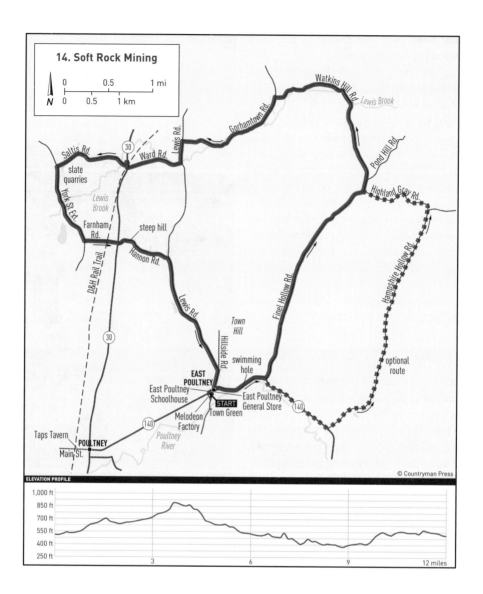

14. Soft Rock Mining

slate quarries

Lewis Brook

York St Ext.

Farnham Rd.

D&H Rail Trail

30

Saltis Rd.

Ward Rd.

Lewis Rd.

30

Gorhamtown Rd.

Watkins Hill Rd.

Lewis Brook

Pond Hill Rd.

Highland Gray Rd.

Hampshire Hollow Rd.

steep hill

Hannon Rd.

Lewis Rd.

Finel Hollow Rd.

Town Hill

Hillside Rd.

swimming hole

EAST POULTNEY

East Poultney Schoolhouse

START

Town Green

East Poultney General Store

140

optional route

Melodeon Factory

Poultney River

Taps Tavern

140

POULTNEY

Main St.

© Countryman Press

ELEVATION PROFILE

1,000 ft
850 ft
700 ft
550 ft
400 ft
250 ft

3   6   9   12 miles

AT A GLANCE Soft Rock Mining: East Poultney and Slate Quarries

DISTANCE: 12 miles
ELEVATION GAIN: 948 feet
MODERATE

0.0 — Park at the East Poultney Green in front of the General Store or at many other spots around the green. Head east on Route 140. Watch for swimming hole pull-off.

0.7 — Left on Finel Hollow Road.

3.1 — Left on Watkins Hill/Pond Hill Roads, then stay left on Watkins Hill Road.

5.2 — Left on Gorhamtown Road.

6.5 — Left on Lewis Road.

6.7 — Right on Ward Road.

7.4 — Right on Route 30 and then an immediate left on Saltis Road. (Note rail trail crossing here.) Enter moonscape.

8.3 — Left on York Street Extension. Second moonscape.

9.3 — Left on Farnham Road. Exit moonscape.

9.7 — Cross Route 30 onto Hannon Road. Short, steep climb.

10.3 — Right on Lewis Road.

11.7 — Right on Hillside Road.

12.0 — Arrive at East Poultney Green.

15

Pleasant Valley

Saxtons River, Cambridgeport, and Brockways Mills, Vermont

DISTANCE: 16.4 miles
ELEVATION GAIN: 915 feet
MODERATE/CHALLENGING
Over the river and through the woods and fields. A delightful ride in pure Vermont countryside.

This is one of those the-more-I-do-this-the-more-I-like-it rides. The back roads are appropriately back, the scenery is nicely diverse, and Pleasant Valley could not be more aptly named. It's a ride worth building a day around.

Start this ride somewhere along Main Street in Saxtons River. There's not a great church/school/post office parking lot. I tend to park down at 37/39 Main Street in front of a not-much-used building in between Main Street Arts and the Post Office and across from where West-minster Street heads south. Main Street is also Route 121, and you'll start by heading west toward Grafton along Route 121/Main Street, which neatly follows

the Saxtons River on your left. This is a relatively high-speed traffic road with not a lot of shoulder, but the river and valley views keep you engaged. About a half-mile from town, at a big bend, notice a gravel pull-off with a trail down to a Vermont River Conservancy public access swim spot in the river. You'll peddle on for a few miles, up for a while then down to the striking stone remnants of a mill on the outskirts of the lost village of Cambridgeport, where you'll take a right on Cambridgeport Road. There were 19th-century wool, saw, grist, and soapstone mills in this village, and this ruin at the corner is all that's left. You've gotten the least pleasant section of the ride out of the way.

Cambridgeport Road soon turns to dirt and you ride along in the wide valley of Weaver Brook. Then you'll start a climb that lasts for a couple of miles before leveling out and rambling through hardwood forest. At almost the top of the climb, there's an elegant, classic farmhouse that's rumored to belong to a Hollywood star. You can't miss it. Then you'll climb a bit more and enter John Dorand State Forest and climb through a small gap at the crest of the ridge—a miniature Smuggler's Notch. Now you start the long descent. Houses appear, farm fields open up, and you wind up in a corner of the lost village of Bartonsville in the town of Rockingham, Vermont.

A quick left and then a right and you're on Route 103 between Bellows Falls and Chester, not lost anymore. Turn right on Route 103 and enjoy a gentle mile-long downhill on a wide shoulder. You won't mind the truck traffic. Turn left on Wil-lems Road and cross the Williams River through the Worrall Covered Bridge.

This bridge was built in 1870 by local master builder Sanford Granger. Of seventeen covered bridges once located in

CROSSING THE SOMETIMES TUMULTUOUS WILLIAMS RIVER THROUGH THE WORRALL COVERED BRIDGE

this town, this is the only original one left. One of those nearby bridges, the Bartonsville Bridge, was destroyed by flooding during Hurricane Irene in 2011 and has since been replaced by a new bridge. It's a sign of commitment to preserving these compelling traditional structures.

The next mile on Williams Road follows the river through a cool, shaded tunnel. You'll appreciate the shade if you're doing this ride on a hot, summer day. At Brockways Mill Road take a right and re-cross the Williams River at a point where the placid flow turns into a tumultuous cataract. You can imagine how this river could eat bridges. Around the corner, at the bottom of the falls, there's supposed

to be an excellent swimming hole. I've never been because the trail down looks challengingly steep, but my son says it's cool.

Head up Brockways Mill Road for a bit of a climb up to Route 103. Turn left and then in a few tenths of a mile turn right on Pleasant Valley Road and start a mellow climb. You'll climb and roll for miles through classic Vermont farmland. Midway it'll get woodsy, you'll pass over a height of land from the Williams River watershed into the Saxtons River watershed, and then you'll start to descend along a string of wetlands which gradually is ponded up at the Saxtons River Recreation Park. I've always considered stopping here for a post-ride swim. Though in the summer of 2021, I found a Facebook conversation where one local resident was asking about leeches. Someone else responded that she had been there with a group and they'd only encountered one leech. I suggest a quick in and out if you decide to swim here.

But leeches aside, this last 3 miles coasting down Pleasant Valley Road is one of the best endings to a ride you can imagine. Goldfinches flit, the slope is gentle and provides just the right speed, and you don't have a care in the world as you merge back onto Route 121 and head back to your car.

DINING OPPORTUNITIES

Saxtons River Market in the village is a good post-ride lunch spot. Good deli, a soup or two usually available, a cafe table or two in the window in front. A popular bike riders' stop.

I would be remiss if I didn't mention the once-awesome snacking opportunity at the **Vermont Country Store**, located back there on Route 103 just about a half-mile past Pleasant Valley Road. Pre-pandemic, this was the place to stop to take advantage of all the food sampling opportunities. Tasting samples abounded. Three-year-aged cheddar, summer sausages, Effie's Oatcakes, whole blueberry jam, pretzels, honey sesame sticks, tapenade, oyster crackers, maple horseradish mustard. You could shamefully assemble an almost complete lunch with samples. Sadly, of course, this tasting buffet has been attenuated by the pandemic. Is it too much to hope that it may return post-pandemic?

If you're heading back through Bellows Falls on your drive, consider the **Moon Dog Cafe** for eccentric and wonderful lunch offerings.

TREASURE HUNT: FIND THIS SPEED LIMIT SIGN AT ONE OF YOUR RIVER CROSSINGS

SWIMMING OPPORTUNITIES

On Route 121 about a half-mile west of Saxtons River, there's **a Vermont River Conservancy (VRC) swimming access point**. The VRC has been active in preserving swimming hole access as an inalienable right for all Vermont residents and visitors. This spot has a nice, not very deep pool, though recent flooding may have tampered with the aesthetics of the place. But there's a nice gravel pull-out, the water quality is excellent, and it's a quick walk from your car down to the gravel bar at water's edge.

There's the swimming hole down in the **Brockways Mills Gorge** for the intrepid few willing to scramble down the steep trail from the parking area on the east side of the road next to the bridge. I've asked around and haven't found anyone who has been down there recently. Report in if you make the descent.

The **Saxtons River Recreation Park** has a small swimmable pond with tannin-stained water and a small sandy beach. You passed it on your descent down Pleasant Valley Road. It'd be a quick way to wash off the sweat if you're good with a quick in-and-out plunge.

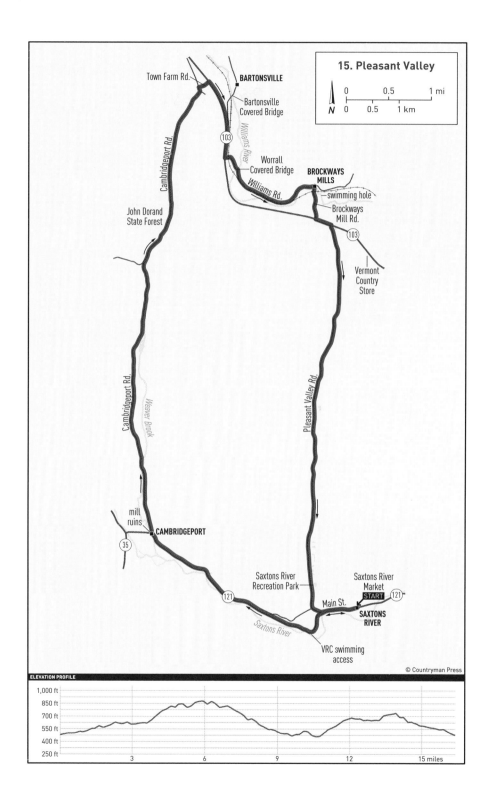

15. Pleasant Valley

BARTONSVILLE
Town Farm Rd.
Bartonsville Covered Bridge
Cambridgeport Rd.
103
Williams River
Worrall Covered Bridge
BROCKWAYS MILLS
Williams Rd.
swimming hole
Brockways Mill Rd.
John Dorand State Forest
103
Vermont Country Store
Cambridgeport Rd.
Weaver Brook
Pleasant Valley Rd.
mill ruins
CAMBRIDGEPORT
35
Saxtons River Recreation Park
Saxtons River Market
START
121
Main St.
SAXTONS RIVER
121
Saxtons River
VRC swimming access

© Countryman Press

ELEVATION PROFILE

1,000 ft
850 ft
700 ft
550 ft
400 ft
250 ft

3   6   9   12   15 miles

AT A GLANCE Pleasant Valley: Saxtons River, Cambridgeport, and Brockways Mills

DISTANCE: 16.4 miles
ELEVATION GAIN: 915 feet
MODERATE/CHALLENGING

0.0 Park in front of 37/39 Main Street in between Post Office and Main Street Arts in the village of Saxtons River, VT. Head west on Route 121 toward Grafton.

2.9 Right on Cambridgeport Road, right before mill ruin.

8.3 Left on Jackson Road and quick right on Town Farm Road.

8.5 Right on Route 103/Rockingham Road.

9.4 Left on Williams Road and pass through Worrall Bridge.

10.8 Right on Brockways Mills Road. Stop on bridge to appreciate cataract.

11.2 Left on Route 103.

11.4 Right on Pleasant Valley Road.

16.1 Merge onto Route 121 and coast back to your car.

16.4 Arrive back in Saxtons River.

16

West River Valley

Newfane and Brookline, Vermont

DISTANCE: 11.8 miles
ELEVATION GAIN: 959 feet
MODERATE

Beautiful river views, a lost unvillage, an exhilarating downhill, a very much found and classic village.

Newfane is the county seat for Windham County, and this ride starts at the imposing, classical Windham County Courthouse. We went to Teddy and Lauren's wedding here recently and the courtroom looks just like it did a century ago—very *To Kill a Mockingbird*. Ample parking on the south side of the green in front of the courthouse. Head south on Route 30 passing the Fat Crow restaurant which you may want to consider for post-ride libations and food. After crossing Smith Brook, turn right onto Bruce Brook Road. And after crossing another branch of Smith Brook, turn left on Browns Road. There's a stately brick Cape on this corner with an appealing swimming pond across the street on your left. Descend along this road, appreciating that you're

not on Route 30 until, alas, you take a right on Route 30, but only for a moment. In a few tenths of a mile turn left on Brook Street and then left on River Road.

Now the pretty backroads flavor that called you to this ride unfolds. This road rises and falls with views of the West River all along the way. About midway, where the bank drops steeply down to the river, look for a rope swing if you're into that sort of thing. After this, you'll pass a sprawling horse farm with miles of fenced pens that look like the board for a labyrinthine computer game. After 2 miles on River Road, take a right on Grassy Brook Road to cross the West River on an iron bridge. (Note the path down to an easy-to-get-to swimming hole on the east bank of the river.)

Just past the bridge you'll pass Hill Road, where you'll come down in about 30 minutes.

Grassy Brook Road follows the sweep of a big bend in the river, past more farms until you cross the namesake brook for this road. Take a left here. (Unless you're up for the challenge of going right and ascending Putney Mountain Road, a 1,000-foot climb.) You're heading up the Grassy Brook valley, a pleasing hidden valley that leads up into the lost unvillage of Brookline, home to about 500 people. There's a town hall up there somewhere and a church, I think. The kids go to school back in Newfane so only an old schoolhouse or two. There aren't a lot of Vermont towns with so little village center. (Actually, find your way to Baltimore, Vermont, for a similarly lost unvillage.) Despite there not being a village, this is a pleasant ride in the company of the gallivanting brook.

At Hill Road take a left. Until now, this ride has been reasonably mellow; you've got two climbs in the second part of the

TREASURE HUNT: THE GRAND WINDHAM COUNTRY COURT HOUSE IN THE CENTER OF NEWFANE

ride. This one is reasonably comfy, only a couple of hundred feet of elevation. And you are rewarded with one heck of a downhill. The pavement is smooth, the road curves, dips and dives, the farm views are soothing and about midway down this hill, you'll start to think, *Wait! We couldn't have climbed this far.* So even though you're returning to a spot you've already been, it feels like you descended more than you climbed.

This ride fits into our category of M.C. Escher rides. You've seen those Escher graphics that somehow trick the eye so that water is flowing downhill in a circle. You know it's physically impossible and you can't figure out how he manages to create the illusion. Similarly, there are bike loops that seem like there's way more downhill than uphill (which is impossible if you're biking a loop—they have to be the same).

This illusion is created because you gently climbed 100 feet along Grassy Brook Road without really thinking you were climbing before you got to Hill Road. This illustrates the mechanical advantage of gently inclined planes. Back at Grassy Brook Road, take a right, cross back over the West River bridge, and instead of taking a left on River Road, head uphill on Radway Hill Road, a steep slog up to Route 30.

At this point, repeat the mantra that *Into each bike ride, some rain must fall.* Not necessarily literal rain, but rather understand that though I aspire to curating perfect rides, sometimes you just have to accept a few flaws. The next mile on Route 30 manages the unpleasant trifecta of being moderately steep, having a minimal shoulder, and there's unusually fast traffic. Grin and bear it. As you start to descend back into Newfane, take a right

TREASURE HUNT: FIND THIS SOMEWHAT MORBID CIVIL WAR MEMORIAL PLAQUE ON THE NEWFANE GREEN

CROSSING THE WEST RIVER AND HEADING TOWARD BROOKLINE

You passed **Fat Crow** in the beginning of the ride. This used to be, hands-down, the best post bike or ski lunch spot in southern Vermont. Incomparably delicious. Then there was a fire—total destruction—and this new restaurant rose on the same footprint. But it was reborn as a dinner restaurant. The food is similarly great, but if you're used to mid-day biking and lunch dining, it won't be available. Open 4 to 9 p.m. Wednesdays through Sundays. Wood-fired pizzas, BBQ, tacos, but everything with a unique twist. Worth planning around when it's open.

on Cross Street, away from mean Route 30, then a left on West Street to enter the village down a lane of crisp white houses with inviting porches, well-tended perennial gardens, and neighbors chatting on the sidewalks. You'll want this idyll to last, but too soon you're back at the Courthouse.

DINING OPPORTUNITIES

There's the **Newfane Store**. Excellent deli menu. Some recent specials included reuben poutine, a banh mi sandwich, and loaded baked potatoes. Taco Tuesdays from 5 to 7 p.m. You'll find something appealing. The green in front of the courthouse is a great spot for a picnic.

SWIMMING OPPORTUNITIES

You passed a great swim option twice back there on the east bank of the **West River on Grassy Brook Road**. Easy access, clear path, avoid the poison ivy, sandy and gravelly beach. Shallow and deep spots and usually not much current.

If you're heading south, there's also a classic swimming hole at the **junction of the West and Rock Rivers** where the road to Williamsville cuts off Route 30. (*There are actually a couple more swimming holes if you're willing to head up the trail along the Rock River.*) If it's a warm summer day there will be a hundred cars parked here so it's really obvious. One caveat, don't leave valuables in your car. In fact, recently, a couple of cars had their catalytic converters cut off while their drivers were swimming here! Is there no shame? But it is a nice swim spot.

IT'S NOT ALL PRETTY LANDSCAPES ON VERMONT BACKROADS

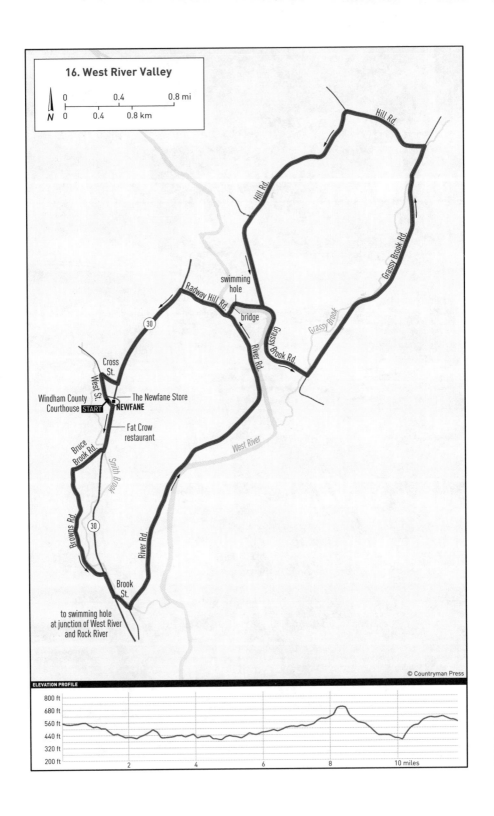

16. West River Valley

N
0   0.4   0.8 mi
0   0.4   0.8 km

Hill Rd.

Hill Rd.

Grassy Brook Rd.

Grassy Brook

swimming hole

Radway Hill Rd.

bridge

30

Grassy Brook Rd.

Cross St.

River Rd.

West St.

The Newfane Store

Windham County Courthouse START **NEWFANE**

Fat Crow restaurant

West River

Bruce Brook Rd.

Smith Brook

Browns Rd.

30

River Rd.

Brook St.

to swimming hole
at junction of West River
and Rock River

© Countryman Press

ELEVATION PROFILE

800 ft
680 ft
560 ft
440 ft
320 ft
200 ft

2   4   6   8   10 miles

AT A GLANCE West River Valley: Newfane and Brookline

DISTANCE: 11.8 miles
ELEVATION GAIN: 959 feet
MODERATE

0.0	Park on the south side of the green in front of the Windham County Courthouse in the center of Newfane. Head south on Route 30.
0.4	Turn right on Bruce Brook Road.
0.6	Turn left on Brown Road.
1.5	Right on Route 30.
1.7	Left on Brook Road.
1.9	Left on River Road.
4.5	Right on Grassy Brook Road, and cross the West River.
5.5	Turn left to continue on Grassy Brook Road.
7.5	Left on Hill Road for a moderate climb.
8.1	Bear left to stay on Hill Road to climb a bit more, followed by a great swoop.
9.9	Right on Grassy Brook Road. Cross back over West River.
10.2	Continue straight, uphill on Radway Hill Road.
10.6	Left on Route 30. Grin and bear it.
11.5	Right on Cross Street then left on West Street.
11.8	Arrive back at Courthouse.

Lost Valley
Putney and Westminster West, Vermont

DISTANCE: 12.6 miles
ELEVATION GAIN: 921 feet
MODERATE/CHALLENGING

A long climb on a paved road and a long descent on an impossibly pretty backroad. This ride makes you feel glad to be alive.

Park at the Putney Central School. This is not to be confused with The Putney School (an independent high school) or the Putney Grammar School (an independent K-8 school). Yes, Putney has a hip, well-educated population (also the site of Landmark College) and it's got a great co-op grocery store as well. There's ample parking at Putney Central just past the school itself on Westminster West Road in Putney.

Turn right out of the parking lot and make friends with this road—you're going to be on it for the next 3.5 miles. This is classically beautiful Vermont farm country, with sprawling meadows on both sides of the road. But it's also classically steep Vermont countryside, so you're going to climb for most of those miles. Appreciate the pavement that makes the climbing a bit easier. This road barely qualifies as a backroad—just

a bit too much traffic nudges it out of backroad status. When you've about had it with climbing, right after High Meadows Farm, you'll take a right off the paved road on South Valley Road. Drift along here for about 0.75 miles and drop into the valley of East Putney Brook. Solar panels accentuate the view of meadows and a distant ridge. At the juncture, bear left to stay on South Valley Road. (To the right is East Putney Brook Road—a different and very cool ride for the next book.)

You'll take a right on Westminster West Road (that little side trip on South Valley was to avoid a hill) and you'll approach the charming village of Westminster West. You'll be reminded to go SLOW, then SLOWER, and finally SLOWEST as you reach the village center. The little school here was the subject of a wonderful progressive education film called *The World in Claire's Classroom,* about a one-room schoolhouse at the end of the 20th century. Look it up. The film asks, What can a classroom of first and second graders in the whitest state in the union teach us about respecting diversity and building community? *The World in Claire's Classroom* documents a veteran public school teacher and her class over the course of a year, with a focus on the children's sustained, in-depth study of another culture. Within this deep and textured exploration, she continually focuses the children's attention back on themselves in relationship to each other, their local community, and the world.

Doesn't this sound like what we need today, in all schools large and small? Claire Oglesby was a brilliant teacher who was widely respected. Remarkable that it happened in this lost little Vermont village.

The signpost at the juncture in the village center, pointing out distances to Minneapolis 1035, Szenstrup 3545,

USEFUL DIRECTIONS IN THE CENTER OF WESTMINSTER WEST VILLAGE

CAN IT GET ANY MORE VERMONT-Y THAN THIS?

Putney 7, and Brienza 4322, suggests that this is the hub of the universe. Time to head toward Putney, and you're not finished climbing yet. Take a sharp left, heading uphill on West Road on well-packed gravel. This climb is Pretty and at the top of the hill it will be Prettier and then you can relax into the Prettiest section of the ride. All that climbing now pays off in a joyful, never too fast, mostly untrafficked gambol down a close-to-perfect backroad. On your left you get maple-tree-framed window views of sun-splashed meadows. (There's a kind of secret network of Nordic ski trails through these meadows in the winter.) On your right, the hills rise up to the Putney Mountain-Pinnacle-Windmill Ridge range which is accessible via a well-maintained set of trails. (This land conservation initiative is a wonderful gift to southern Vermonters. Read more about it at www.windmillhillpinnacle.org.)

As you descend, you'll drop into the valley of one of the branches of Sacketts Brook and transition from sun-splashed meadows into a narrow dappled hemlock glen. Back out into meadows, then back into hemlock glen. All this while mostly just gliding downhill without much effort. This is what all those "Life is Good" t-shirts are referring to. At the bottom of this glide, you'll merge with Tavern Hill Road and then quickly cross the main stem of Sacketts Brook. (Take note: this is where you want to return for a post-ride swim.)

After passing a few stately homes and strings of barns, you'll be back at Westminster West Road. Take a right and you'll be back at Putney Central School in no time.

DINING OPPORTUNITIES

For fine dining, **The Gleanery** in the center of Putney is Vermont farm-to-table at its finest. Their website describes it: "Our

guiding principle is that everything that you see in The Gleanery has been carefully selected for being artisanally made. The ingredients in the dish, the dish itself, the table below it; everything is there because a person wanted to create it. We foster an environment that exalts anyone who takes pride in their craft."

For simpler grab-and-go salads, sandwiches, and cold drinks, you can't beat **The Putney Co-op**. It's been around since before the idea of hip cooperative grocery stores was a thing. The Putney Co-op was founded in 1941 to make the acquisition of food more possible for local residents during the shortages of World War II. Great place to shop and a pleasing little cafe and deli. It'll give you that warm and fuzzy feeling of doing good while you shop or dine.

SWIMMING OPPORTUNITY

The Culvert, right across from the Putney Grammar School on Hickory Ridge

TREASURE HUNT: FIND THIS SAGE ADVICE AS YOU APPROACH THE VILLAGE OF WESTMINSTER WEST

Road (not Putney Central School), is a popular local swimming hole. You passed it a few miles back. Sackett's Brook tumbles through a big culvert into a deep emerald pool right next to the road. Really short distance from parking to immersion. Crystal-clear water, sandy and gravelly bottom, always bracingly chilly, nothing creepy. Access it via a steep footpath on the left side of the brook.

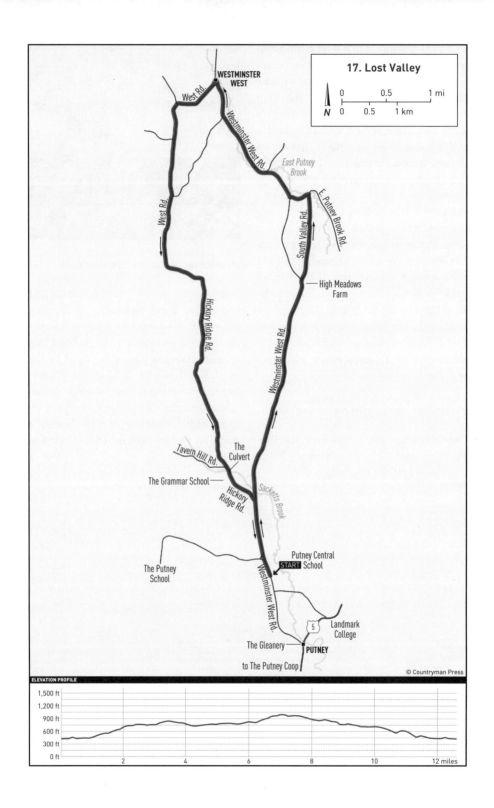

17. Lost Valley

WESTMINSTER WEST

West Rd.

Westminster West Rd.

East Putney Brook

E. Putney Brook Rd.

South Valley Rd.

West Rd.

High Meadows Farm

Hickory Ridge Rd.

Westminster West Rd.

Tavern Hill Rd.

The Culvert

Sacketts Brook

The Grammar School

Hickory Ridge Rd.

Putney Central School

START

The Putney School

Westminster West Rd.

Landmark College

5

The Gleanery

PUTNEY

to The Putney Coop

© Countryman Press

ELEVATION PROFILE

1,500 ft
1,200 ft
900 ft
600 ft
300 ft
0 ft

2   4   6   8   10   12 miles

AT A GLANCE Lost Valley: Putney and Westminster West

Distance: 12.6 miles
ELEVATION GAIN: 921 feet
MODERATE/CHALLENGING

0.0 — Start at Putney Central School on Westminster West Road in Putney. Head north on Westminster West Road.

3.4 — Right on South Valley Road.

4.3 — Bear left to stay on South Valley Road.

4.5 — Right on Westminster West Road. Go Slow, Slower and Slowest as you approach the village.

6.2 — Left at the prominent road signs in center of village on West Road.

6.8 — Bear left to stay on West Road. Don't consider any turns off West Road for the next 4 miles. Somewhere along here West Road becomes Hickory Ridge Road.

11.3 — At juncture with Tavern Hill/Black Locust Road, continue straight on Hickory Ridge Road South.

11.8 — Right on Westminster West Road. You were here an hour ago.

12.6 — Arrive back at Putney Central School.

Hollow and Heights

Weatherhead Hollow and Guilford Center, Vermont

DISTANCE: 12.2 miles
ELEVATION GAIN: 1129 feet
CHALLENGING
A classically beautiful Vermont countryside ride with all the pastoral fixings. Classic elevation profile and really simple directions.

We like to start this ride at the corner of Guilford Center and Weatherhead Hollow Roads in Guilford. There's a little pull-off between Guilford Center Road and the Broad Brook. We park here because this means you end this ride with a glorious twisty downhill. Or to make it about 3 miles longer, you can start at the Guilford Country Store in the village of Algiers.

Why is the biggest village in the eastern part of Guilford called Algiers? The story goes that in the old days, there was a running poker game with players from Brattleboro, Guilford, and Marlboro. Seems like the Guilford card players were always cleaning up at these games. On one particularly hot night when the Guilford players fleeced everyone, one

of the Brattleboro players said, "You Guilford boys are nothin' but a bunch of Algerian pirates!" This was a reference to pirates from Algeria who at that time would prey on ships passing through the straits of Gibraltar in the Mediterranean Sea. Hence, Algiers.

From the aforementioned corner, head south on Weatherhead Hollow. This isn't the kind of deep-clefted hollow you find in West Virginia, but rather more of a broad vale hollow. Regardless, it couldn't be more beautiful. Open meadows and working farms abound between two well-defined ridges on either side of the hollow. You'll pass the Guilford Country Fairground about a mile or so down. The road is mostly flat, a little roll-y, lightly trafficked, though you're gradually climbing to a height of land about 3 or 4 miles south.

A Note on the Guilford Country Fair: I studiously avoid most county fairs these days. They seem mildly seedy, with boring monster truck spectacles, cotton candy that gives me the shivers, and carnival rides that I now know too much about to feel comfortable on. But the Guilford Country Fair is charming and worth considering. There's a good old-fashioned tug-of-war competition, complete with dousing with fire hoses, there's medieval costumed revelry, much of the food is from local farms, and Guilford's great local music scene is on display. It's in a beautiful meadow on one side of the hollow. Feels like the best combination of the good old days and the good new days.

The meadows abate, the forest closes in. Ferny glades crowd the maple-shaded road. You climb over the height of land separating the Broad Brook from the Keets Brook watershed and you cruise down to Weatherhead Hollow Pond. This is one swim option for this ride. Right at the end of the pond, and right before the

Franklin Farm (great place to purchase hamburger, salad dressing, maple syrup, and other farm products), take a right on Sweet Pond Road. For the next couple of miles, you're climbing steadily. There's a nice alternation of climbing followed by flat-ish sections in the beginning. You'll pass a beautiful old schoolhouse, attractive Vermont farmhouses, little tucked away meadows. You've got the upper stretch of Keets Brook to keep you company. And, in the fall, keep your eyes open for the bright orange-yellow Chicken of the Woods shelf fungi on some of the old trees below the road.

After the entrance to tiny Sweet Pond State Park about two-thirds of the way up, the climb is steady. I consider this whole climb from Weatherhead Hollow Road till you crest out at Abijah Prince Road kind of foreboding. It's a climb of 450 feet and can get a bit tedious, but it's beautiful enough to keep me somewhat distracted. Once you've reached the top, there's a mile or so of relatively flat ridgetop cruising. Then comes the payoff. The next 3 miles of downhill are "Oh my God beautiful"—one of the prettier places in Windham County. The goldfinches flit and white-tailed deer bound through well-tended meadows; the view stretches for miles. Sometimes I get choked up over the pure loveliness of it all. The woods close in and you'll eventually merge onto Stage Road and continue your downhill flight until you enter the perfect lost village of Guilford Center. Stop awhile and linger.

Guilford Center: My wife and I have done a lot of workshops right here in this village and there's really more than meets the eye here. It has all the essential components—the church, the meeting house, the historical society (very active), and the eminent Broad Brook Grange. A bit down Carpenter Hill Road, there's

CRUISING THE SHORE OF WEATHERHEAD HOLLOW POND

TREASURE HUNT: PEEK THROUGH THE WINDOW TO FIND THIS INTERIOR VIEW JUST ON THE OUTSKIRTS OF GUILFORD CENTER

promised dessert of this ride. With the babbling Broad Brook as your faithful companion, you'll coast the next twisty and turn-y couple of miles back to your car. It's gentle enough to not have to touch your brakes much, but steep enough to be exhilarating. It's the perfect end to a perfect ride.

DINING OPPORTUNITIES

Hurray! for the country store revitalization movement in northern New England. The **Guilford Country Store** is a shining example of this movement. In many little towns, the country store is the only store in town, and it functions as the diner, pub, old-timers-sitting-around-and-chewing-the-fat venue, business lunch, or meet your neighbors place. The country store was revitalized by The Friends of Algiers Village, a local non-profit with help from Mrs. Kramer's middle school students at the Guilford Central School. The Harrisville General Store in New Hampshire served as one of the design inspirations for this renovation, so see if you can identify some of the similarities.

the Old Brick Schoolhouse #1. Unlike in most Vermont towns, most of Guilford's 14 original district schoolhouses are still intact. This one is owned by the historical society. Peer in the windows to get a glimpse of the desks and original slate blackboard.

Across from the schoolhouse is the entrance to the Weeks Forest—a lovely walk with an engaging trail guide created by the Conservation Commission and 6th graders from the school. (Place-based education at its finest!) If you get far enough up this trail, you'll get to the site of the Old Mineral Springs—it was a spa where you came to "take the waters." Before the schoolhouse in the meadow, there's the newly crafted Guilford Community Natural Playscape. Find your way down to the tiny beach on the babbling brook.

Enough rhapsodizing. Hop back on your bike and continue on down Guilford Center Road, past the road up to the Town Offices and the school. Here's the

There are always chicken kabobs, delicious salmon, kale salad, great sandwiches. You basically can't go wrong here, except that sometimes it's hard to find a table. It's a destination lunch spot when Brattleboro folks want to get out into the country. They just don't agree to play poker here. The Philly steak-cheese sandwich is better than the originals. It's a remarkably cheery place with remarkably good food.

Or, if you have a little grocery shopping to do, head back up Route 5, which turns into Canal Street, to get your post-ride snack at the **Brattleboro Food Co-op**. There's a cafe with fine soups and sandwiches. This Co-op is really one of the great co-ops in New England, with every organic and whole food imaginable,

SCHOOLHOUSE #1 JUST DOWN CARPENTER HILL ROAD FROM GUILFORD CENTER

complete with hippie checkout girls and boys. Gilfeather turnips and heirloom tomatoes abound. At one point in the late 20th century, the hip scene in America was described as being most alive in Berkeley, Boulder, and Brattleboro. You can see why when you shop at the Co-op.

SWIMMING OPPORTUNITIES

You passed **Weatherhead Hollow Pond** earlier in your ride. It's a bit marshier than I tend to like for post-ride dips— lots of lily pads, pickerelweed, and other emergent vegetation—but it's right there and easily accessible. There's a reasonably unmarshy swim access at a little gravelly spot at the south end. You'll bike right by it, and you can assess its appeal.

If marshy doesn't appeal to you, head back down Guilford Center Road to Algiers Village. Just down **Broad Brook** Road, the brook passes underneath I-91 and tumbles across the slate belt. At the point where the road crosses Broad Brook, there are nice spots both upstream from the bridge and down below the falls. Parking for three or four cars here. This is one of those pristine streams with silver-green water, so the water is always chilly and brilliantly refreshing. We were here once when someone's car had just been broken into, but that was only once. Worth the bit of risk, I think.

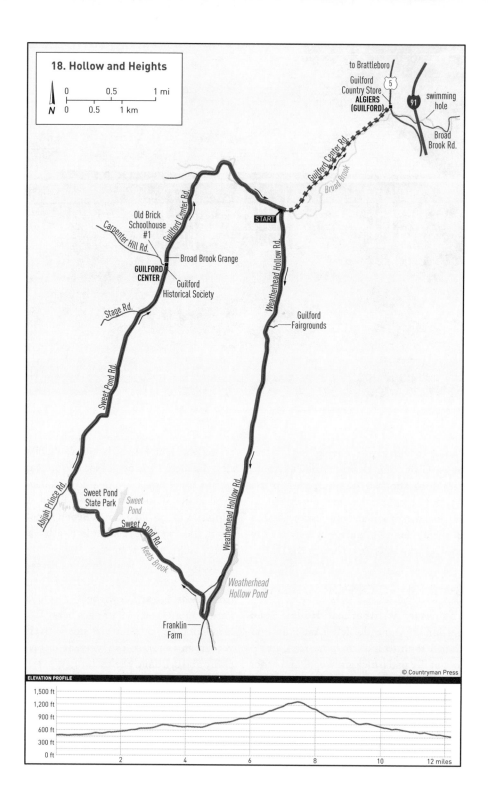

18. Hollow and Heights

N

0   0.5   1 mi
0   0.5   1 km

to Brattleboro

Guilford
Country Store
**ALGIERS
(GUILFORD)**

5

91   swimming
hole

Broad
Brook Rd.

Guilford Center Rd.

Broad Brook

Old Brick
Schoolhouse
#1

Carpenter Hill Rd.

Guilford Center Rd.

Broad Brook Grange

**GUILFORD
CENTER**

Guilford
Historical Society

Stage Rd.

START

Weatherhead Hollow Rd.

Guilford
Fairgrounds

Sweet Pond Rd.

Abijah Prince Rd.

Sweet Pond
State Park

Sweet
Pond

Sweet Pond Rd.

Keets Brook

Weatherhead Hollow Rd.

Weatherhead
Hollow Pond

Franklin
Farm

© Countryman Press

ELEVATION PROFILE

1,500 ft						
1,200 ft						
900 ft						
600 ft						
300 ft						
0 ft						
	2	4	6	8	10	12 miles

AT A GLANCE Hollow and Heights: Weatherhead Hollow and Guilford Center

DISTANCE: 12.2 miles
ELEVATION GAIN: 1129 feet
CHALLENGING

0.0 Start at the junction of Guilford Center Road and Weatherhead Hollow Road. Small gravel pull-off on the Broad Brook side of the road. Head south on Weatherhead Hollow Road. (Alternative starting point at the Guilford Country Store in Algiers.)

4.6 Just past Weatherhead Hollow Pond and before the Franklin Farm, turn right on Sweet Pond Road. Climb for a while.

7.2 Crest out, almost at the top, at junction with Abijah Prince road. Continue on Sweet Pond Road. The hills are alive with the sound of music.

9.3 After a long downhill, turn right on Guilford Center Road, pass through the perfect lost village of Guilford Center and tumble down along the Broad Brook.

12.2 Arrive back at your car at the junction with Weatherhead Hollow Road.

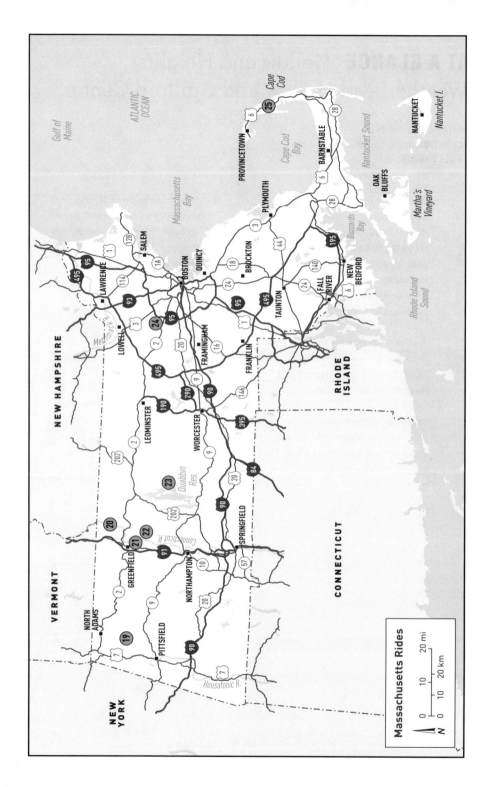

MASSACHUSETTS RIDES

(West to East)

THE ASHUWILLTICOOK TRAIL HUGS THE SHORE ALONG CHESHIRE RESERVOIR

19

Ashuwillticook Trail

Adams and Cheshire, Massachusetts

DISTANCE: 17.1 miles
ELEVATION GAIN: 916 feet
MODERATE

A remarkably interesting ride in an unexpected place. Diverse terrain and one of the more glorious sections of bikeable road in Massachusetts.

Start this ride in the ample parking lot of the Adams Visitor Center on Hoosac Street in downtown Adams, Massachusetts. It doesn't look very backroads-y, but get ready for an intriguing ride.

A Historical Note on the Mill Towns of the Hoosac River Valley, Adams and North Adams: When I went to college in this area in the late 1960s, these mill towns symbolized American industrial decay. Factories were empty, unemployment was high, tourism was nil. This was in stark contrast to the industrial boom in the valley in the late 19th century. Transforming cotton grown in the south to cloth was big business. The Berkshire Cotton Manufacturing Company (all those massive mill buildings around you) was the second-largest employer in the county. The completion of the

Hoosac Tunnel in 1873, an 8-mile passage through the Hoosac Range, connected western Massachusetts to the world. Immigrants poured in. There were nine different ethnic groups, and sermons were preached in five languages. When cotton manufacturing moved south and overseas in the 1950s and '60s, Adams and North Adams slipped into the doldrums, only to be revived with the arrival of the Massachusetts Museum of Modern Art, the North Adams Heritage State Park, and the creation of this rail trail. If someone had told me that North Adams would become a hip-i-fied tourist destination in the 21st century, (see The Porches), I wouldn't have believed them.

Before I discovered this ride, I wouldn't have given Adams a second thought as a possible bike destination. Take this ride and discover otherwise. Out of the parking lot, head south on the rail trail. You're following the channelized Hoosac River through the remains of the industrial boom. Old railroad sidings, crumbling buildings, and mill housing line the trail—it feels Dickensian. But as you head out of town, the chortling river starts to dominate, the ruins disappear, the forest closes in, and you climb slowly but steadily up the valley. After Harbor Road you bend away from Route 8 and it feels like a back road. Then, surprise, you're in a marshy wonderland. The Hoosac dawdles and meanders here for miles, pickerelweed and cattails flourish, herons lift off from trailside pools—unexpected. At about 5 miles, you cross Church Street in Cheshire. You'll be back here in about half an hour. Another mile and you cross Route 8 and enter the next unexpected phase of the ride, Cheshire Reservoir.

Cheshire Reservoir was created in the 1860s to store water to run the mills where you started back in Adams. Textile mills depended on water power (until

HARD NOT TO STOP AT DIANE'S TWIST AT THE
INTERSECTION OF THE ASHUWILLTICOOK TRAIL AND THE
APPALACHIAN TRAIL

scene. After a bit of a steep climb, take a right on Lanesboro Road to roll up and down high above the lake with great views out to the east.

Take a left on Route 8 for just a moment and then zigzag your way back down toward the rail trail with a right on Richmond Street, a left on Dean Street, a right on Depot Street, and then a left on Railroad Street. This is a pure Americana neighborhood with a number of Trump 2020 banners. Do these make this neighborhood more American or less?

Once back at the Rail Trail crossing, a stop at Diane's Twist is de rigueur. Diane looks to be in her 80s and she runs a mean little snack bar all by herself with a remarkable panoply of offerings—overstuffed sandwiches, baby steamed hotdogs with lots of fixings, ice cream sundaes, twists. She gets a lot of business because she's at the intersection of the Rail Trail and the Maine to Georgia Appalachian Trail after it descends from Greylock and starts the ascent of the Hoosac Range. Fun to chat with the through-hikers carbing up or enjoying a banana split. At least get yourself a cold Diet Pepsi so you can enjoy this idiosyncratic spot.

Continue a bit past Diane's and then bear left on Main Street/Wells Road. The next couple of miles are the draggy part of the ride. It's a back road, but it manages the perfect trifecta of a moderately steep climb, no shoulder, and aggressive traffic. Eventually, you'll top out and start to enjoy the mondo views to the west and east—a glimpse of what's to come. At about 13 miles, descend to Route 116, take a right, and then pretty soon a left onto Henry Wood Road/Bucklin Road.

that was replaced by steam engines) and volumes of water oscillated during the year. There were ample amounts of water in winter and spring and diminished amounts in summer and fall. Industrial production needed water to happen year-round, and the mill owners needed a dependable way to store winter and spring water to use in summer and fall. Hence, this reservoir, which you are now appreciating as you pedal hard-by the shore. It's unusual to have a bike trail so close to the water's edge, with unobstructed views out across the water. Cooling breezes from the south and grand views up to the Greylock range. Midway down the reservoir, take a right on Farnams Road through a nice little park with fishing access and ladies in beach chairs. It's a pleasing summery

This is the main act, the reason you came on this ride, la crème de la crème. Sprawling farm meadows snuggle up right to the road's edge—no hedgerows or a border of trees to peer through. The farm buildings gleam red, the clouds tromp across the blue sky, and the hills are alive with the sound of music. With uninterrupted views of Mt. Greylock to the west, and the long ridge of the Hoosac Range on the east, it's breathtaking. The climb is a bit arduous for a mile. Then you level out in pastoral bliss and start a descent into what looks like a hidden valley. (The road is now called East Road.) Hard not to feel joyous. But then the road gets bumpy, you round a bend, and you're back in mini-mansion land—the fleetingness of a dream. Even more unexpected is Susan B. Anthony's Birthplace Museum—nicely preserved in early 19th-century style with an excellent interpretation of her life and the women's suffrage movement. Did you know she said, "Bicycling did more to emancipate women than anything else in the world?" What a great thought to end this ride.

There are now numerous ways to drop down (steeply!) into Adams. My recommendation: Just past the museum, take a left on Meadow Street, a cute little gravel road that looks like a dead end. It weaves down through old mill housing along a brook, and then take a left on East Hoosac Street. (As you descend Meadow Street notice the white cliff excavations on the side of Greylock—the domain of Specialty Minerals. Among other minerals mined here, think talc, baby powder, Johnson & Johnson, big problem.)

At the intersection with Summer Street, you'll want to proceed straight ahead to the visitor center, but for some odd reason Hoosac Street is closed to bicycles. Therefore, take a left on Summer Street, a right on Weber Street, a right on Winter Street (imposing, slightly scary mill building on your left), and then a left on Hoosac Street back to your parked car. What a wonderful, strange trip it's been.

DINING OPPORTUNITIES

For pure, old world ambiance, trundle down Depot Street to **AJ's Trailside Pub**. You passed it early in the ride. The door makes you feel like you're entering a

THE LONG BUT BREATHTAKING CLIMB UP HENRY WOOD ROAD WITH VIEWS OF MT. GREYLOCK TO THE WEST AND THE HOOSAC RANGE TO THE EAST

speakeasy. It's dark and crowded inside with tattooed guys lining the bar, the Red Sox are on the big screen, Bud, Coors Lite and PBR are on tap. We had the deconstructed pierogis special one time here, which was surprisingly good. I recommend sitting outside on the nicely shaded patio so you can watch the bikes go by. My suggestion for a post-ride quaff—a shandy made with two-thirds lager, one-third ginger ale, and a splash of lemonade on ice. Very refreshing.

When my wife used to come to Adams to shop the fabric outlets about 20 years ago with her four young boys, she always stopped at **Pedrin's Dairy Bar** just north of town on Route 8. It has the same time travel back to the 1950s feel as AJ's. More high camp than high cuisine, and local folks love it.

For more time travel shock, head to the food trucks or cafes in the **Mass MOCA complex in North Adams**. In the summer of 2021, there was a pop-up Georgian restaurant (as in post-Soviet Union Georgia) in the courtyard with an esoteric menu. At **Lickety Split**, inside the museum, you can get gourmet sandwiches, Thai salads, breakfast bowls. Very urbane and very unlike the menu at Pedrin's or AJ's.

SWIMMING OPPORTUNITY

More surprises. Within the industrial sprawl of Adams, there's a popular, almost pristine, cool swimming hole. Hard to believe. Brisk, green, refreshing—it even has a splashy waterfall. From swimmingholes.org, here are the directions to **Bellevue Falls**.

From the intersection of Route 8 and Route 116 in the center of Adams, travel south on Route 8 for 0.7 miles and take a left onto Leonard Street. Follow Leonard Street for 0.2 miles and turn right onto Bellevue Avenue and enter the Bellevue Cemetery. Take every right-hand turn while on the cemetery road and park at a small parking area beside the picket-type fence. Follow the well-worn path down the hill to the main swimming area.

If you follow these directions exactly, you'll find it. Worth the search.

TREASURE HUNT: IT'S HARD TO MISS THIS ONE—A UNIQUE BLEND OF UTILITY AND ART

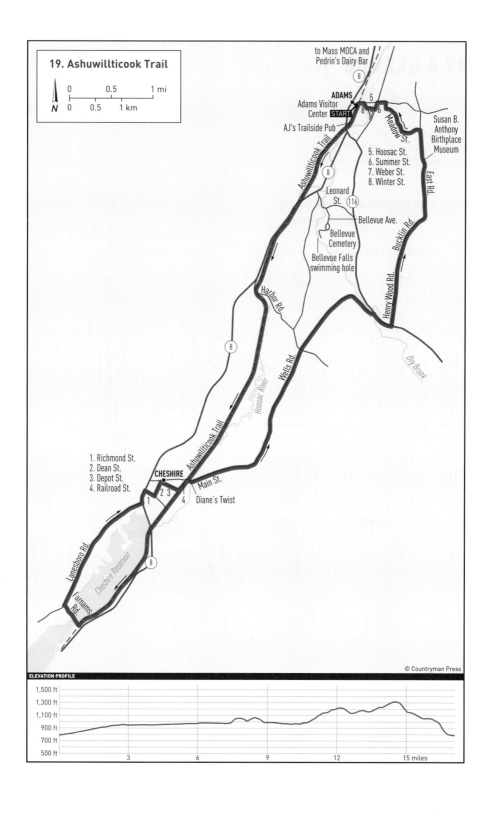

19. Ashuwillticook Trail

N 0 — 0.5 — 1 mi
0 — 0.5 — 1 km

to Mass MOCA and
Pedrin's Dairy Bar

(8)

ADAMS
Adams Visitor
Center START
AJ's Trailside Pub

Ashuwillticook Trail

(8)

Leonard
St. (116)

Meadow St.

5
8 7 6

5. Hoosac St.
6. Summer St.
7. Weber St.
8. Winter St.

Susan B.
Anthony
Birthplace
Museum

East Rd.

Bellevue Ave.

Bellevue
Cemetery

Bellevue Falls
swimming hole

Bucklin Rd.

Henry Wood Rd.

Dry Brook

Harbor Rd.

(8)

Wells Rd.

Hoosac River

Ashuwillticook Trail

1. Richmond St.
2. Dean St.
3. Depot St.
4. Railroad St.

CHESHIRE

2 3 1

1 4

Main St.

Diane's Twist

Lanesboro Rd.

Cheshire Reservoir

(8)

Farnams
Rd.

© Countryman Press

ELEVATION PROFILE

1,500 ft			
1,300 ft			
1,100 ft			
900 ft			
700 ft			
500 ft	3	6	9	12	15 miles

AT A GLANCE Ashuwillticook Trail: Adams and Cheshire

DISTANCE: 17.1 miles
ELEVATION GAIN: 916 feet
MODERATE

0.0 Park at the Adams Visitor Center on Hoosac Street in downtown Adams, MA. Head south on Ashuwillticook Rail Trail.

5.6 Cross Route 8. Continue on Rail Trail along Cheshire Reservoir.

7.1 Right on Farnams Road.

7.4 Right on Lanesboro Road.

9.0 Left on Route 8.

9.1 Quick zigzags—right on Richmond Street, left on Dean Street, right on Depot Street, left on Railroad Street.

9.8 Mandatory stop at Diane's Twist. Continue past Diane's on Church Street.

9.9 Left on Main Street/Wells Road.

13.3 Right on Route 116/Savoy Road.

13.6 Left on Henry Wood Road/Bucklin Road. Becomes East Road.

15.6 Susan B. Anthony Birthplace Museum. Continue on East Road.

16.0 Left on Meadow Road. (Looks like dead end.)

16.6 Left on East Hoosac Street.

16.7 Quick zigzags—left on Summer Street, right on Weber Street, right on Winter Street.

16.9 Left on Hoosac Street and then left onto rail trail to car.

17.1 Arrive back at Adams Visitor Center parking.

20

Old Man River and the Devil

Northfield, Gill, and Satan's Kingdom, Massachusetts

DISTANCE: 29.3 miles
ELEVATION GAIN: 1861 feet
CHALLENGING

Two shorter rides or one long very diverse ride.
Enjoy the pastoral beauty of the Pioneer Valley
on both sides of the Connecticut River and
explore a little-known wilderness area on the
Massachusetts/Vermont border.

If you want to do the whole enchilada (both the southern and northern sections of this ride), or just the southern section, then start at the wonderful Four Stars Brewery tucked away at 508 Pine Meadow Road, south of Northfield village. If you want to just do the northern, wilder section of the ride, then start at the parking lot for the Pioneer Valley Regional High School on F. Sumner Turner Drive. This description will assume you're doing both. The southern section, while beautifully pastoral, is marred slightly by some state highway stretches, but redeems itself with the variation between tucked down by the river and being surrounded

by meadow and farm splendor. There's a great lost village along the way. The northern section involves a section of woods road, is a bit rough and root-y for a couple miles but is fine for hybrid or gravel bikes. And it's evocatively creepy.

Depart Four Stars Brewery and take a right on Pine Meadow Road. You're starting here so you can have a cold, locally brewed beer in beautiful surroundings at the end of the ride. If you're here before the brewery is open, there'll be a big empty parking lot.

Pine Meadow Road heads south through cultivated potato fields. You'll alternate between wide open spaces and shady tunnels just above the mighty Connecticut. As you cross Four Mile Brook, consider stopping to walk upstream a bit to see the beautiful arched stone tunnel that the brook flows through under the railbed. You'll pass a boat launch/recreation area, and somewhere in here the road name changes to River Road. At about 3 miles, you'll pass under the vaulted infrastructure of the French King Bridge. Just around the corner take a quick detour down to the bike bridge over the Miller's River, giving you another view of the French King Bridge up high over the confluence of the Miller's and the Connecticut.

Disappointingly, you're not biking across this bike bridge, but instead heading uphill on Dorsey Road to take a left on Route 2. This is as close to interstate-like traffic on a two-lane highway that you'll encounter. Heavy traffic, big trucks, everyone going 65 mph. There's a very wide shoulder though, and you do get to cross the dramatic French King Bridge. It's about a mile and a half of concentration before you take a right on Pisgah Mountain Road.

After this right, you'll take another quick right to stay on Pisgah Mountain

PASSING UNDER THE FRENCH KING BRIDGE ON RIVER ROAD BEFORE RIDING OVER IT

Road, and you're quickly far away from all that traffic. This road rises a bit and then drops into a little hemlock notch, traversing back down to the river valley below. Dark hemlock lostness and then you pop back into potato fields—a wonderful quick transition from traffic to lostness to cultivation. At the bottom of the notch you're back on a different River Road. There's a fairly long climb in here, then the road changes back to pavement and you gambol along through farms stretching down to the river with mountain views in the distance.

At about 8 miles you'll slide into Gill, a perfect lost village. People who live in Amherst have never heard of it. Off the beaten path, lovely, and has one of the best restaurants around. Note the odd

construction of the cute town library. It's made with cinder blocks because a local manufacturer of cinder blocks donated the money and materials for construction of the library. I challenge you to find another cinder block town library in New England.

Take a right on Main Road and up and down your way north. You'll pass Upinngil Farm and numerous other farms replete with sheep, cows, and chickens. You'll eventually skirt the edge of the Northfield/Mount Herman (NMH) campus—a fine boarding school that all parents wish they could send their children to. Fun to detour up and knock around this beautiful campus.

Off to the right you'll see a giant installation of solar panels. This contrasts interestingly with the view of Northfield Mountain, on the other side of the valley, which hosts one of the larger pump storage facilities in New England. This is a contrast between 21st-century and 20th-century energy production. The pump storage project was a massive land excavation and landscape manipulation project built in the 1960s. A giant reservoir was created on the top of the mountain and water is pumped from the Connecticut River up into the reservoir at night, during low power demand hours, to basically create a battery of potential energy. Then during the day, during peak demand hours, water flows steeply downhill through massive pipes and through a buried hydroelectric facility inside the mountain. Massively expensive and resource consumptive as compared to the photovoltaic arrays here on this side of the river. Hopefully this illustrates an evolution in our electricity production strategies over the past 50 years. (Note: Northfield Mountain has a great Nordic skiing trail network, open during winters when climate change hasn't diminished the normal amount of snowfall in north central Massachusetts.)

Your arrival at Route 10 is a decision point. If you're going to continue to do the northern section of the ride, you're going to turn left uphill and then right on F. Sumner Turner Road to pass Pioneer Valley Regional School. If you're only doing the southern section of the ride, turn right on Route 10, cross the river, then head south on Route 63 to take a right on Pine Meadow Road.

Let's continue north. The upcoming forested section is spooky and provides a great contrast to the rest of this ride. It's a great ride unto itself if you want something shorter. Pass up between the high school and the recreational fields. Take a left on Bennett Brook Road and then right on Route 142, but only for a moment. Look for the quick left turn at the bottom of the hill onto Old Vernon

Road. Right away, you're on a causeway, sunny marshes on both sides, while you enjoy sheltered riding along the pine-lined, sun-dappled road. It's marshes for miles, with turtles sunning, herons lifting off, otters fishing in the recesses you can't see. Eventually you'll pass a few houses and the paved road ends. Suburbia quickly transforms into a slightly eerie four-wheel-drive, hemlock-shaded woods road. Poof! Wilderness—in Satan's Kingdom, an undeveloped Massachusetts State Forest. The riding gets a bit stony at times, pleasantly challenging. After about a mile you'll come to a clearing with a timeworn cabin and you'll feel like you're in the recesses of the Adirondacks, or like you've stumbled into an H. P. Lovecraft story. Then more marshes and hemlock. Too soon, you're back in paved suburbia for a moment, bear left at the junction onto

THE PAINFUL BEAUTY PART OF THIS RIDE THROUGH MEADOWS ON POND ROAD

Scott Road and then you're back in the deep woods for another quarter of a mile. This oscillation between suburbia and wilderness gives this section a Where am I? feeling.

As you approach the sunlit, paved section of road in the distance, look for a granite post indicating you're crossing the Massachusetts/Vermont state line. I still feel that little frisson of excitement from my youth of crossing a border—like driving into Canada but with less oomph. Now you're back on pavement, in the rural burbs of Vernon, Vermont, still home to the long-to-be-dangerously-radioactive-but-now-closed Vermont Yankee Nuclear Power station.

You T out onto Pond Road, take a right, and then prepare yourself for the beauty of the next 1.5 miles.

Pond Road glides gracefully downslope. Lime green meadows sprawl out on either side of you, a range of mountains defines the far horizon, goldfinches flit about, and it's all a bit too much, overfilling, painfully beautiful. It's amplified by the contrast that you were just deep in wilderness and now here's the shock of

TREASURE HUNT: YOU HAVE TO TURN DOWN DEPOT ROAD IN THE LOST VILLAGE OF NORTHFIELD STATION TO FIND THIS UNIQUE DISPLAY OF MUGS

human-tended cultivation. Both immersive, both with their own unique provocation of the senses.

Take a right on Route 142. There's the classic, house-ells-sheds-barns-connected-on-and-on Vern-mont Farm on the right and a cute little old brick schoolhouse on the left. In the *Vermont Gazetteer* this is referred to as the lost village of South Vernon. Then back across the state line into the lost village of Northfield Station. (For a quick detour, take a left on Old Depot Road to take you down to the old depot.) Past Old Depot Road, continue on Route 142 for another 100 yards and take West Northfield Road on a bridge across the railroad tracks. Back into real farm country.

The next couple of miles are as flat as a pancake and traverse the same rich, river-deposited, alluvial Connecticut River valley soils as earlier. Famous for growing tobacco, asparagus, strawberries, and all manner of garden vegetables. It can be unshaded and hot along here, so take advantage of the shade of the two railroad trestles that you cross underneath on this still active train line. And if you're doing this in summer or fall, you might get the treat of seeing the harvesting of one of the unexpected products of these flat, rich soils—lawn turf. Can this be any more different than the spooky hemlock wilderness of Satan's Kingdom?

At the end of the farm fields, you have to climb out of the floodplain up onto the kame terraces, old glacial deposits of sand and gravel on the side of the valley lining what used to be old Lake Hitchcock. Lake Hitchcock filled much of the Pioneer Valley at the end of the Pleistocene Glacier era and where streams entered the lake, they deposited sand and gravel. Over the next mile you'll climb about 200 feet up across two different levels of kame terrace and then take a left on Route 142. Notice the vast sand and gravel pit operations on both sides of the road, reaping the harvest of these glacial deposits. After the gravel pits, there's a quick down and up, past the turn to Satan's Kingdom, and then a left on Bennett Brook Road back to the high school. If you're just doing the northern part, end here. If you're headed back to Four Stars Brewery, don't turn into the high school but continue straight to take a left on Old Bernardston Road and then bend around to come out to take a left on Route 10. It's an unpleasant, slightly uphill slog across the Connecticut River and then a right on Route 63 south.

To minimize the amount of time you're spending on big roads, take a quick left on Lucky Clapp Road, then a right on Captain Beers Plain Road for a quiet neighborhood break. Cross Route 63 and jog right on Jewett Road and then left on Upper Farms Road for a quiet farm break before you have to take a left on Homer Road to rejoin Route 63 to the right. My friend Chris refers to this as the etch-a-sketch version of this ride because you could just stay on Route 63 the whole time. But in the spirit of finding back-roads, I like this option. There's another mile of Route 63, with a wide shoulder, until you can leave the busy world behind and take a final right onto Pine Meadow Road. It's all gravy for the last couple of miles, flat or slightly downhill until the towering hops on the right signify the end of the ride.

BREWERY OPPORTUNITY

The Brewery at Four Stars Farm is a great addition to the local craft brewing scene. It's located on an expansive hops farm (17 acres!), so it's fun to gaze out at the vertically growing hops as you sip a cold lager. They provide fresh hops to breweries across New England. The beers are sprightly fresh, and there's a wide range of seating options. The Bine Cutter IPA is citrus-y and delicious. Cozy outdoor couches in patio shade. Picnic tables with umbrellas, Adirondack chairs—lots of options. Dare I say it feels a bit Californian? In a good way?

DINING OPPORTUNITIES

The sandwiches at **Mim's Market** are dependably quick and good. In season, **Northfield Creamie** always has a line out front. The vanilla chocolate creamie twist is a trip down memory lane for me.

For casual chic, head back across the river to the **Gill Tavern**, mostly a dinner place but they open by 4 p.m. This is one of our go-to places, and we have designed bike rides to take advantage of this unusually fine restaurant. Great bar with local microbrews on tap. The food is locally sourced, the blue-cheese garlic bread is pungent, and there's always a few inventive things on the menu. The open, tiny kitchen allows you to watch the chef in action.

SWIMMING OPPORTUNITY

If you're up for a bit of exploration to a cool swim spot, head over to Bernardston, Massachusetts. Just after you cross I-91 and the southbound access road, there's a gravel parking area on your left with a trail heading off at the back corner. It's a steep little downhill, but the trail twists nicely away from the road so that by the time you're down at the **Fall River**, you're tucked out of sight. There's a nice sandy entrance into the water, the water quality seems close to pristine, and there's an ample pool to dabble around in. It'll feel like your own little secret.

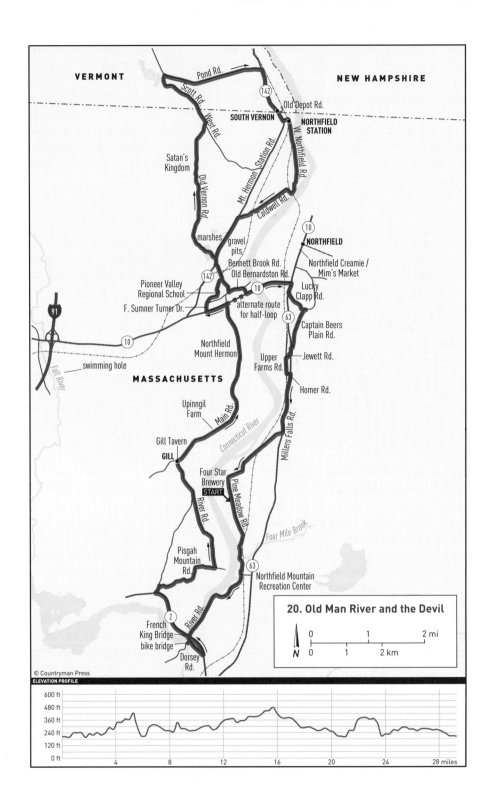

VERMONT NEW HAMPSHIRE

Pond Rd.

Scott Rd.

West Rd.

142

Old Depot Rd.

SOUTH VERNON NORTHFIELD STATION

W. Northfield Rd.

Satan's Kingdom

Mt. Hermon Station Rd.

Caldwell Rd.

Old Vernon Rd.

10

NORTHFIELD

marshes

gravel pits

Bennett Brook Rd.

Old Bernardston Rd.

Northfield Creamie / Mim's Market

Pioneer Valley Regional School

142

10

Lucky Clapp Rd.

F. Sumner Turner Dr.

alternate route for half-loop

63

Captain Beers Plain Rd.

91

10

Jewett Rd.

swimming hole

Fall River

Northfield Mount Hermon

Upper Farms Rd.

Homer Rd.

MASSACHUSETTS

Upinngil Farm

Main Rd.

Millers Falls Rd.

Connecticut River

Gill Tavern

GILL

Four Star Brewery

START

Pine Meadow Rd.

River Rd.

Four Mile Brook

Pisgah Mountain Rd.

63

Northfield Mountain Recreation Center

2

River Rd.

French King Bridge
bike bridge

Dorsey Rd.

20. Old Man River and the Devil

N

| 0 | | 1 | | 2 mi |
| 0 | 1 | | 2 km | |

© Countryman Press

ELEVATION PROFILE

600 ft
480 ft
360 ft
240 ft
120 ft
0 ft

4 8 12 16 20 24 28 miles

AT A GLANCE Old Man River and the Devil: Northfield, Gill, and Satan's Kingdom

DISTANCE: 29.3 miles
ELEVATION GAIN: 1861 feet
CHALLENGING

0.0 — Start in the parking lot of Four Stars Brewery at 508 Pine Meadow Road in Northfield, MA. Turn right and head south.

3.0 — After you pass under the French King Bridge, head uphill on Dorsey Road.

3.4 — Turn left on busy Route 2/2A.

4.8 — Right on Pisgah Mountain Road and then another quick right to stay on Pisgah Mountain Road.

6.2 — At bottom of descent, bear left. Road is now called River Road.

8.3 — Arrive Gill Village and turn right on Main Road.

11.4 — Arrive Route 10. **Decision point.** To just do the southern section, turn right here and rejoin directions at 24.7 miles below. To do the northern section, turn left here.

11.8 — Right on F. Sumner Turner Drive.

12.5 — Left on Bennett Brook Road.

12.8 — Right on Route 142/Mount Hermon Station Road.

12.9 — Left on Old Vernon Road.

14.6 — Paved road ends, continue straight ahead and enter Satan's Kingdom on four-wheel-drive road.

15.5 — Bear left on West Road amidst a bit of suburbia. When this road crosses the Vermont border, it becomes paved and is now Scott Road.

16.7 — Right on Pond Road.

18.5 — Right on Route 142/Fort Bridgeman Road.

19.5 — Left on West Northfield Road.

20.3 — At Schell Bridge Road on left, West Northfield Road becomes Caldwell Road. Continue South.

21.0 — Left to stay on Caldwell Road.

22.0 — Left on Route 142.

continued

22.9 Left on Bennett Brook Road. (Turn into high school if just doing northern loop.)

23.5 Left onto Old Bernardston Road and bend to right to intersect Route 10.

23.8 Left on Route 10.

24.7 Right on Route 63/Miller's Falls Road.

24.8 Left on Lucky Clapp Road.

25.3 Right on Captain Beers Plain Road.

26.0 Cross Route 63 and turn right on Jewett Road. Down to a quick left on Upper Farms Road.

26.5 Left on Homer Road, and then a quick right on Route 63.

27.6 Right on Pine Meadow Road.

29.3 Arrive back at Four Stars Brewery.

21

Time Travel
Turners Falls and
Deerfield, Massachusetts

DISTANCE: 18.4 miles
ELEVATION GAIN: 855 feet
MODERATE

A trail of two towns and three rivers. Try to figure out the circuitous interplay of the Connecticut, Deerfield, and Green Rivers, which you'll cross on a diversity of bridges. And enjoy slipping through a time warp into two completely different 18th- and 19th-century historical villages.

Start this ride at the ample parking lot of the Great Falls Visitor Center in Turners Falls, the largest of the three villages of Montague, Massachusetts. Stop into the visitor center before or after your ride. There's a striking three-dimensional model of the Connecticut River Valley and really expertly created dioramas of the flora and fauna of the valley. The "Great Falls" refers to the significant cataract on the Connecticut River that was the reason for the industrial development of Turners Falls. The falls were dammed and a power canal created to provide the energy for a wide array of industrial mills in the 19th and early 20th century. The canal is still intact, the mills mostly abandoned, with some revitalized, including the buildings for the visitor center.

A paean to Turners Falls: this is a great ride, in part because it starts and ends in Turners Falls, a somewhat lost small city that you've probably never been to. Lost less geographically than lost in time. It's frozen in the 1950s, as illustrated by the Shady Glen Diner on your left on Avenue A just as you come across the Connecticut River Bridge. All of downtown is the perfect movie set for retro movies. Think *It's a Wonderful Life* or the more recent *Stranger Things* series. Have your bike day include a meal and a wander through neighborhoods and the park along Barton Cove. Turners Cove is the country cousin of next door Greenfield and the more affluent towns further south in the Pioneer Valley. As the property values in those places rise,

THE BIKE TRAIL FOLLOWS THE POWER CANAL THROUGH THE MILL DISTRICT IN TURNERS FALLS

Turners Falls has started to experience its own Brooklynification.

From the parking lot, find the path to the right of the visitor center that descends to the Canalside Rail Trail. Take a left and pass through the time warp into the industrial 19th century. The path follows the power canal. On your left is old residential mill housing; across the canal on your right are the old, mostly abandoned, extensive mill buildings. Looking for an artist's loft or a big space for a tech start-up? This may be the place. The industrial architecture along here—elevated walkways, large culverts, building ventilation structures, and brick crenulations are fascinating. The flow of the water in the power canal gives you momentum heading south. You'll pass the Brick and Feather Brewery as you cross 11th Street. Keep that in mind for later.

The Rail Trail goes for longer than you'd imagine, at least a couple of miles, and turns into Depot Street. At the Depot Street/Montague City Road intersection, take a right and head south to cross the Connecticut River bridge. Bear left at the end of the bridge into a lost corner of Greenfield, separated from the main part of town by the long ridge of Rocky Mountain Park.

This neighborhood, for the next few miles, defined by the confluence of Green, Deerfield, and Connecticut Rivers was known as Cheapside. It was a mill village populated by German immigrants who worked in the Russell Cutlery factory that opened in 1836. It was busy with wharves and docks until boat transportation was supplanted by the railroad. You'll encounter a chunk of rail infrastructure later in the ride.

Montague City Road becomes Cheapside Street, you'll pass under a big railroad trestle, and then you take a right on Routes 5/10. A lot of traffic, a reasonably good shoulder, and good furniture shopping along here. In half a mile, keep your eyes peeled for Petty Plain Road on your left which takes you on a pedestrian bridge over the Green River. Continue on Petty Plain Road for the only significant climb of the ride and past a cemetery. Take a left on Wisdom Way. Look for the Harvest Moon Farmstand on your left, which prompts a detour into biking and weather predictions.

When planning bike outings during the summer, you're often confronted with the problem of how to deal with the forecast of a 30% to 40% chance of isolated or scattered thunderstorms. The attitude I've developed, after canceling rides because of this forecast, is to now proceed full steam ahead. Ergo, I was on a ride in this area when we got to the corner of Petty Plain Road and Wisdom Way. The thunder was rumbling and the cold downdrafts were announcing the storm's imminence. We looked for a place to ride out the storm and, lo and behold, there was the Harvest Moon Farmstand, empty of vegetables and a completely suitable rain shelter. It torrented for about 20 minutes, then the sun came out and we continued on the ride with sun sparkling off the rain-drenched trees. So my maxim is: *Most thunderstorms pass quickly and there's almost always an interesting place to get out of the rain.*

Past Harvest Moon, cross the interstate and take a left on Upper Road. From the urban edge of Greenfield, you'll now rise into orchard land on the hillsides above the floodplain of the Deerfield River. If it's late summer or early fall, it'll be hard to resist the ripening apples barely an arm's length from the road. Or stop in at Clarkdale Fruit Farms when you see a 10-foot apple to snag a nice tart Macintosh or a peach, plum, pear, or handful of cherries. It's a nice lilting ride

GLASSY SKY REFLECTIONS AS YOU CROSS THE DEERFIELD RIVER MIDWAY ON THE RIDE

along the orchard edges, climbing gradually for the first mile, leveling off, and then swooping downhill for the last mile to a bridge across the Deerfield River.

Left on Stillwater Road, cruise along the river leaving orchard world and entering floodplain farm world to see ... Wait! What's that in the field on both sides of you? Looks a lot like marijuana, but it's hemp. Take a left on Mill Village Road and you're surrounded by reminders that the Connecticut River Valley (though this is actually the Deerfield River Valley right here) is the vegetable basket of New England. Potato fields, followed by expanses of day lily cultivation, patches of asparagus gone to seed, rows of corn, and then stunning weeping willows—a garden of Eden. After a couple of miles of farm fields, you climb a bit, and poof, you're back in the late 18th century at the head of the long, maple-alléed Main Street of Deerfield.

The village is home to Historic Deerfield, "an outdoor museum that interprets the history and culture of early New England and the Connecticut River Valley. Visitors can tour twelve carefully preserved antique houses dating from 1730 to 1850." There are world-class collections of regional furniture, silver, textiles, and other decorative arts on display if that's your thing. In addition to the museum buildings, there are numerous private homes impeccably preserved so it feels less like touristy Sturbridge, more secretive and breathtaking. There's also tony Deerfield Academy with similarly beautiful architecture and greens, the cozy Deerfield Inn, and the appealingly cute buildings of the Bement School, an independent K-8 school.

At the end of Old Main Street, bend right and then take a left on Routes 5/10 heading north. It's a bit of a rude awakening to make the quick transition from 18th-century placidness to fast-paced 21st-century traffic. But there's only about a mile of this before you take a right on River Road and climb a bit until you get to the incredibly expansive East Deerfield Rail Yards, yet another distinctly different world on this historic ride. Bear left on McClelland Farm Road and then take a quick left onto the lower end of the Canalside Rail Trail. You'll swoop down through shady forests and then cross the long Connecticut River bridge back into Turners Falls. At the end of the trail, take a quick left and then a right on Rod Shop Road to pass by a boarded-up elementary school built in 1884 and more waiting-to-be-restored mill buildings.

APPLES ABOUND ADJACENT TO THE ROAD NEAR CLARKSDALE FRUIT FARM

Left on Solar Avenue, right on Montague City Road, and then to avoid some of the city sprawl, take a right on Turnpike Road and then a left on Walnut Street for a golf course moment. Turn right on Montague City Road, which turns into Avenue A and you're back in the *It's A Wonderful Life* section of Turners Falls. Cruise up Avenue A back to your car.

DINING OPPORTUNITIES

In keeping with the theme of Brooklynification, find the **Five-Eyed Fox** tucked away on 3rd Street. Easy to miss, worth finding. It's owned and operated by women. There's a great little bar, a good place for Sunday brunch, or a post-ride lunch or snack, very hip. Food is locally sourced, homemade, eccentric, maybe a bit pricey, but you're also paying for the atmosphere.

The **Brick and Feather Brewery**. We haven't been here, but it's on my shortlist of go-to places. A few web comments: "My favorite brewery in western Mass. Amazing, hazy, full-bodied, complex IPA's." And: "Lawrence George pours me a hazy-gold sample from the tank and passes it to me in a small glass. It is a bold and flavorful take on an American pale ale." I'm sold.

If you're heading over toward Greenfield, consider stopping at the **People's Pint**, another fine local brewery, local foods purveyor, and bicyclist hotspot.

SWIMMING OPPORTUNITY

The Green River Swimming and Recreation Area on the north side of Greenfield is the perfect place for a post-ride

TREASURE HUNT: FIND THIS COLONIAL DOORWAY ALONG MAIN STREET IN HISTORIC DEERFIELD VILLAGE

swim. It's worth the price of admission ($8 for nonresidents) and yes, it'll be filled with toddlers, splashing children, and picnicking parents, but it's also classic Americana. There's a little riverside beach, lots of picnic tables, a concession (chips, $2 hotdogs), and the water quality is great. Since it's a section of dammed up river, there's a gentle flow of water through the pool and the upriver Green River water is pristine. This place always makes me happy.

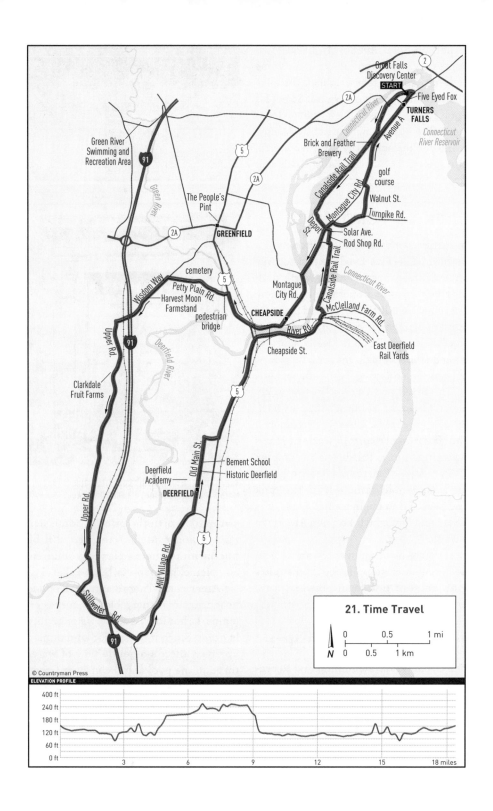

21. Time Travel

0   0.5   1 mi

0   0.5   1 km

ELEVATION PROFILE

400 ft
240 ft
180 ft
120 ft
60 ft
0 ft

3   6   9   12   15   18 miles

© Countryman Press

AT A GLANCE Time Travel: Turners Falls and Deerfield

DISTANCE: 18.4 miles
ELEVATION GAIN: 855 feet
MODERATE

0.0 Park in the Great Falls Discovery Center parking lot in Turners Falls, just off Avenue A on 2nd Street. Descend past the visitor center to Canalside Rail Trail.

0.1 Left on Canalside Trail. At end of trail continue onto Depot Street.

2.2 Right on Montague City Road heading south. Cross Connecticut River Bridge.

2.8 Left to stay on Montague City Road, which becomes Cheapside Street.

3.9 Right on Routes 5/10.

4.4 Left on Petty Plain Road and cross pedestrian bridge.

5.1 Left on Wisdom Way.

5.9 Left on Upper Road. Enter orchard world.

9.3 Left on Stillwater Road.

10.2 Left on Mill Village Road. Enter farm world.

11.9 Bear left on Old Main Street. Enter 18th-century village.

12.9 Bear right and then left on Routes 5/10. Back to 21st century.

14.2 Right on River Road.

15.1 Left on McClelland Farm Road, then quick left on Canalside Trail.

16.1 Right on Rod Shop Road then left on Solar Avenue.

16.3 Right on Montague City Road and quick right on Turnpike Road.

16.8 Left on Walnut Street.

17.3 Right on Montague City Road which becomes Avenue A.

18.4 Arrive back at Great Falls Center parking.

22

Rattlesnake Gutter

Montague and Leverett, Massachusetts

DISTANCE: 15 miles
ELEVATION GAIN: 1006 feet
CHALLENGING

A couple of pristine lost villages and a unique geologic feature make this one of the more intriguing bike rides in north central Massachusetts. Don't do this ride unless you're ready for the steep, gravelly descent of the Gutter—more like mountain biking than backroads biking. But really worth it.

"Books you don't need, in a place you can't find." This trademark saying for the Montague Book Mill captures the essence of this ride. I drove past the village of Montague for more than 30 years before I finally figured out where it was. And I'd always heard about the Book Mill, but it was even lost-er than the village. However, *Now that I've found you, I won't let you go.* We always take at least one bike ride originating here every season; the biking is elegant and the browsing, listening, and gnoshing at the Book Mill are unequaled. Perched above the Sawmill River, the combination of views and dining options is unique.

Park in the upper lot, across the road from the Book Mill, so you're out of the way. But remember to lock your car. My wife had money stolen from her pocketbook here once. Head south into Montague Village. Just past the green, turn left onto South Street, which will take you out to Route 63. A quick right/left zig and zag (right on 63, left onto Ripley Road), where you'll cross railroad tracks and then climb slowly up toward Leverett. I've never encountered a car on this shaded, pleasant lane. After a few miles you'll see a closed-off road heading steeply up to the left as the road you're on tumbles down to the Leverett Road. Dismount, navigate the barrier, and walk your bikes uphill a bit to slide past the Montague Retreat Center. This keeps you off a trafficked road for a bit longer, though you eventually have to descend to it on a bit of Chestnut Hill Road. Take a left onto Leverett Road, and head up along the Sawmill River.

In the lost village of North Leverett, don't be tempted to turn on Cave Mill Road, but instead continue on up another mile to Old Coke Kiln Road. (No road sign here.) A right here, then a left on Hemenway Road which bears left to become Mill Yard Road, and now you're approaching the cool part of this ride. (If the bridge across the Sawmill River is not passable, turn around and take a left to go up Hemenway Road to Rattlesnake Gutter Road.) After a short steep hill, you're going to take a right on Rattlesnake Gutter Road. It's gravelly and casually maintained, so get ready to climb for a while.

However, before you settle into the climb, you've got to check out an inviting little swimming hole. Once you're on Rattlesnake Gutter Road, you'll cross a bridge across a stream, nice waterfall on the right, and look for the grassy, bikeable lane heading upstream on the left. Follow it for a couple hundred yards to a clearing with a bench. Dismount, disrobe, and find your way down to the charming pools in this amiable stream. A sandy bottom, shallow warm water. What's not to like?

Back on Rattlesnake Gutter, you'll climb a couple hundred feet up through hemlocks to the top of the ridge. Vaulted cliff faces rise to your right and then you enter the notch at the top—craggy, eerie, other-worldly. Pitch downhill on an old town road that's stony but ride-able with the steep-sided gutter on your right. (Last time we were here in August 2021, the torrential summer rains had eroded gullies into the top section of this descent. You'll need to dismount to avoid the gullies, and you might have to walk your bike for the first quarter-mile.) The bottom of the gutter is lost in a cacophony of angular boulders. There looks like there should be a stream down there somewhere, but you can't see into the depths. Raven caws echo off the cliffs. You've entered the world of H. P. Lovecraft.

H. P. Lovecraft was a supernatural/ science fiction/horror writer in the early part of the 20th century, the Stephen King of his day. Many of his stories are set in these north central and northwestern Massachusetts hollows. At the end of dirt roads, where the forests crowd out all the sunlight. Where moldering houses and barns rot back into the landscape as evil lurks within. Whenever I'm a bit lost on a Berkshires backroad, I get that little shiver up my spine of Lovecraftian creepiness.

The spookiness gradually subsides as the cliffs pull back, the road levels off, and a bit of a stream appears on the right. Soon you're back into the friendly, UMass Amherst rural burbs of Leverett.

JUMBLY TALUS SLOPES LITTER THE LOWER SECTION OF RATTLESNAKE GUTTER

Spookiness subsides as groovy-ness ascends with the Peace Pavilion at the bottom of the Gutter. Take a right on Montague Road and head northwest for about a mile until you're back on civilized Route 63.

After about a mile on Route 63, you'll take a left down Reservation Road, a steep gravel road along the edge of the Mount Toby Reservation. (No road sign, rather a "this road is not maintained in winter" sign.) Mount Toby is a prominent little peak that sticks up out of the surrounding valley and has a vast network of bikeable roads and hiking trails that we haven't quite investigated yet. At the bottom of

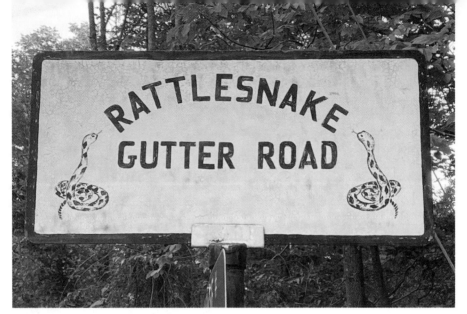

TREASURE HUNT: FIND THIS SIGN AT THE END OF YOUR DESCENT DOWN THE GUTTER

this steep descent, you'll pass a scenic marshy area with great views up toward the mountain, then you'll climb very steeply up the other side to first a trailhead and then a suburban neighborhood.

At the next junction, you take a right onto Route 47, and then a quick left on Fosters Road which drops you down to Meadow Road, along the river and through floodplain farms.

The floodplain farms of the Connecticut River Valley are the "breadbasket" of New England. Though rather than wheat, these farms produce asparagus, cabbage, strawberries, potatoes, pumpkins, tobacco a bit further south, lots of other vegetables, and lawn sod. If you're doing this ride during strawberry season, you may be in luck.

Dally up through these beautiful farms and meadows, bearing right at a juncture to stay on Meadow Road until you cross the Sawmill River (the same river you may have dipped in 45 minutes ago) and take a right on Greenfield Road. Notice the cool cascades in the river next to you and appreciate why this

was a valuable mill site. (Keep your eyes open during this short climb. Last time we were here, a humongous black bear crossed the road in between my wife and me following her not far behind. The bear just missed the back of her bike by about 10 feet. Quite unexpected.) Then, voilà! You're back at the Book Mill.

DINING OPPORTUNITIES:

The Book Mill houses **Lady Killibrew's Tavern and Cafe**, the **bookstore** itself, **Turn It Up**—a used CD/DVD/record store—and **The Alvah Stone**, a hip restaurant. Leave time to take advantage of at least three out of the four of these. For lunch, or just a cold beer, the Lady Killibrew is the lost cafe you're always hoping to find. Pressed sandwiches, gluten-free options, herbal teas, scones, slightly tattered hippie servers, and lots of odd indoor and outdoor seating with waterfall views.

The Watershed Restaurant at the other end of the complex, down around back, is cozy and a bit more elegant. Great farm to

OUT OF THE GUTTER AND INTO THE FERTILE RIVER FLOODPLAIN FARMLAND

THE BOOK MILL IS A WHOLE LOST VILLAGE UNTO ITSELF
TO EXPLORE AT RIDE'S END

table options, a British village pub inside, and outside one of the nicest waterfall-side places to eat in New England. As they say, "If you were dining any closer to the water, there would be fish in your lap."

SWIMMING OPPORTUNITIES:

Back there on the upper reaches of the **Sawmill River.** We usually wait until the end of the ride to swim, but this is so perfectly located at the mid-point of the ride that it's silly not to take advantage of it when you're there.

There's also a nice beach at **Lake Wyola State Park** in Leverett, back up past where you were biking earlier. Not as sparkly as New Hampshire lakes, but a pleasant spot to wash off the grit and sweat from your ride.

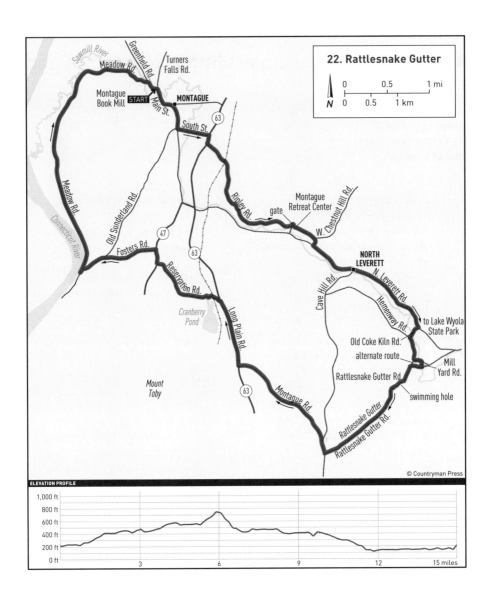

22. Rattlesnake Gutter

Sawmill River
Meadow Rd.
Greenfield Rd.
Turners Falls Rd.
Montague Book Mill
START
Main St.
MONTAGUE
63
South St.
Montague Retreat Center
gate
Ripley Rd.
W. Chestnut Hill Rd.
Meadow Rd.
Old Sunderland Rd.
47
Fosters Rd.
63
Reservation Rd.
Connecticut River
NORTH LEVERETT
N. Leverett Rd.
to Lake Wyola State Park
Cave Hill Rd.
Hemenway Rd.
Cranberry Pond
Long Plain Rd.
Old Coke Kiln Rd.
alternate route
Rattlesnake Gutter Rd.
Mill Yard Rd.
swimming hole
Mount Toby
63
Montague Rd.
Rattlesnake Gutter Rd.
Rattlesnake Gutter Rd.

© Countryman Press

ELEVATION PROFILE

	3	6	9	12	15 miles

1,000 ft
800 ft
600 ft
400 ft
200 ft
0 ft

AT A GLANCE Rattlesnake Gutter: Montague and Leverett

DISTANCE: 15 miles
ELEVATION GAIN: 1006 feet
CHALLENGING

0.0 Park in the upper parking lot across from the Book Mill Complex on Greenfield Road in Montague, Massachusetts. Head south staying on Main Street, past the Town Common until . . .

0.6 Left on South Street.

1.0 Right on Route 63/Federal Street and then a quick left onto Ripley Road.

2.8 When Ripley turns sharply right and downhill, dismount, go around the gate and walk uphill 100 yards, continue on Ripley Road.

3.1 Right on West Chestnut Hill Road.

3.2 Left on West Leverett Road.

4.8 Right on Old Coke Kiln Road.

5.0 Left on Hemenway Road.

5.3 Hemenway bends to the left and becomes Mill Yard Road.

5.4 Right on Rattlesnake Gutter Road. This road climbs and soon turns into an unmaintained road and crests out at the top of the Gutter. The downhill can be rough, but it's very cool.

7.3 Turn right on Montague Road.

8.6 Turn right on Route 63/Long Plain Road.

9.4 Left on Reservation Road. Drop steeply, pass Cranberry Pond, then climb steeply.

10.4 Right on Route 43/Montague Road and then a quick left on Fosters Road.

11.2 Bear left on Old Sunderland Road.

11.5 Right on Meadow Road. Appreciate the difference between the Gutter and these expansive floodplain farms.

14.2 Bear right to stay on Meadow Road.

14.8 Turn right on Greenfield Road, and in the wink of an eye you . . .

15.0 Arrive at the Book Mill.

23

The Hidden World of Quabbin
Petersham and Dana, Massachusetts

DISTANCE: 14 miles
ELEVATION GAIN: 918 feet
MODERATE

A foray into the closely guarded and somewhat mysterious Quabbin Reservation. A visit to the capital of Lost Villagedom in New England, Dana Center, along lonely old roads. This ride lies between being for hybrid/gravel bikes and for mountain bikes.

Quabbin Reservoir and Park is the major water supply for the city of Boston and other municipalities. It was created between 1928 and 1940 by damming the Swift River valleys and flooding out most of the four towns of Dana, Prescott, Enfield, and Greenwich. In addition to the more than 25,000 acres of reservoir, the park contains more than 50,000 acres of protected watershed land. The reservoir and park are very strictly managed to preserve the quality of the drinking water. As a result, Boston's municipal water is one of the highest quality water supplies in the country. Biking is allowed on some of the old town roads abandoned when the reservation was created and they provide some of the most intriguing backroads biking in New England. This ride takes advantage of a small number of them.

Access to the park can be gained through a number of gates that circle the outer edge of the park. Start this ride at Gate 40, about 4 miles south of the Petersham Town Green on Route 32A/Hardwick Road, where there's parking for about 10 cars. Please review all the dos and don'ts on the bulletin boards here. Past the gate, follow the old Dana Road south and west. The intriguing thing about riding in Quabbin is that you're riding on the old asphalt town roads. Some of them are still in reasonable condition but most are crumbling and turning back into gravel roads. But you can sense the existence of old homes and farmsteads in the maintained meadows along the way. (For context see the great children's book about the creation of Quabbin: *Letting Swift River Go,* by Jane Yolen.)

Around 2 miles, you'll arrive at Dana Common, the capital of Lost Villagedom in New England. The town green and most of the cellar holes of the buildings (the town hall, the school, the hotel, the church) are all maintained. Most of the stone walls and old fence posts are intact. The buildings were all razed or moved, and the cemetery remains of all the town cemeteries were relocated to a central graveyard. Dana Common is the only one of the town centers that wasn't flooded. All the others are submerged under the waters of the reservoir. Easy to get the strong spooky sense of a once-thriving village. Very *Brigadoon*-ish. Browse the interpretive panels showing the old buildings and wonder what it was like leaving a home that had been in the family for generations.

YOU'LL NEVER ENCOUNTER A CAR ON THESE ABANDONED TOWN ROADS NEAR THE LOST VILLAGE OF DANA

Continue southwest on Dana Road, that used to lead to Greenwich Village, one of the flooded village centers. You'll pass over a marshy drainage, and the road will be chunky in places. Sometimes easier to ride the grassy mid-strip rather than either of the gravely double tracks. You'll eventually descend to an outhouse maintained mostly for boaters and a side lane down to the edge of Quabbin. Mandatory to head down here to get a glimpse of the massive expanse of this reservoir. Even though those sandy expanses of shoreline beckon to you, swimming is strictly verboten in Quabbin. And you'll note that boaters are only allowed to be on shore for a maximum of 10 minutes to use the facility. Stringent watershed protection!

Dana Road now bends to the left, southeast, and climbs a ridge. Don't take either of the grassy lanes that turn off to the right. Gradually you'll descend to a fishing access area and cross a small dam that separates Pottapaug Pond from the main reservoir. The backroads wildness ends here. After the dam, Dana Road becomes Hell Huddle Road (a historic name for pauper settlements) and is paved; you continue south to Greenwich Road, where you turn left. You're at the southern end of the loop and will now gradually head back north.

After about a half-mile, you'll turn left on Mellon Road and climb for a while. You're still traveling through protected lands along here, so it's house-free and almost has the same lost feeling as Dana Road. At some point you'll pass over the massive pipeline that carries the water to Wachusett Reservoir and then on into Boston, but there won't be any visible sign; it's way below you. At 9 miles you have a choice. You can take a right on Breen Road, which will take you out to Route 32A, or you can continue on

Mellon Road, which is now a four-wheel-drive forest road. It's a bit grassy and rough, fine with hybrid bikes, but the most mountain bike-y mile of the loop.

At 32A take a left. After a bit of a climb, enjoy a mile-long swoop down to a right on what is also called Dana Road. In the old days this road would have crossed 32A and reached Dana Center, where you were an hour ago. (It's possible to just stay on 32A north back to your car, but more interesting to take this additional loop.) Right on Dana Road for a half-mile, left on Carter Pond Road for another half-mile, and then left on Woodward Road. Once you're on Woodward Road, you enter into a magical little world, completely unexpected. Flower-filled ledges on the right, a forest with the understory trimmed out, a beautiful pond and marshy meadows, storybook cottages—the remnants of the lost village of Nichewaug. This is the reason

for backroads biking—you come around a corner and pass through a portal into a timeless and faraway place. Once you get back to 32A, turn right and there's a bit of climb to get back to your car at Gate 40.

DINING OPPORTUNITY

There's only one choice for a post-ride lunch and it's a great choice. **The Petersham Country Store** has operated continuously since 1840. Its Greek Revival building is right in the center of the village. And the village itself is elegant—grand houses spread out around a long green. Couldn't feel more transporting. This might be what Dana Center felt like before it was deconstructed.

The food here is excellent. Small but interesting deli menu—really fresh and prepared on the spot. We had an excellent clubhouse sandwich and the signature salad with greens, sweet potato, goat

TREASURE HUNT: YOU MAY HAVE TO SEARCH A BIT TO FIND THIS COBBLE STONE WALL NEAR DANA COMMON

cheese, brown rice, bacon, almonds— uniquely delicious. This food here is equal to the other revived country stores in Guilford and Peru, Vermont, and Harrisville, New Hampshire.

SWIMMING OPPORTUNITY

Water, water everywhere, but not a place to swim. All those miles of sandy shore on Quabbin are alluring, but swimming is verboten. Such a shame. And we haven't found a really good swim spot in the area. However, one cool, knee-deep place is relatively close. From Gate 40, go south on 32A and take the first left on Glen Valley Road. Go about a mile east to just before the road crosses a bridge. Small pull off on the right side. Short trail down to a pool in the **East Branch of the Swift River**. Nice little sandy beach, enough water to lay down in and get refreshed. Cardinal and monkey flowers along the edges of the stream in August. Quite a pretty little spot, but not a place to dive in.

"WATER, WATER, EVERYWHERE, BUT NOT A PLACE TO SWIM" ON THE QUABBIN SHORE

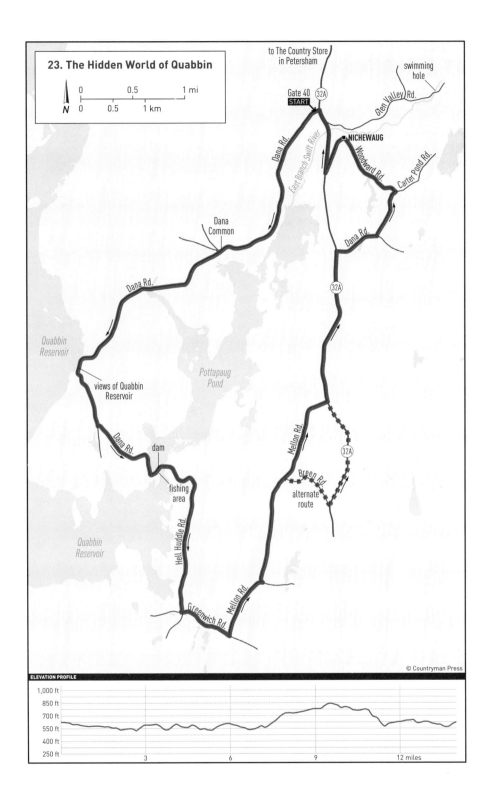

23. The Hidden World of Quabbin

0   0.5   1 mi
0   0.5   1 km
N

to The Country Store
in Petersham

swimming
hole

Glen Valley Rd.

Gate 40
START   32A

NICHEWAUG

Dana Rd.

Woodward Rd.

Carter Pond Rd.

East Branch Swift River

Dana
Common

Dana Rd.

Dana Rd.

32A

Quabbin
Reservoir

views of Quabbin
Reservoir

Pottapaug
Pond

Mellon Rd.

32A

Dana Rd.

dam

Breen Rd.

alternate
route

fishing
area

Quabbin
Reservoir

Hell Huddle Rd.

Greenwich Rd.

Mellon Rd.

© Countryman Press

ELEVATION PROFILE

1,000 ft
850 ft
700 ft
550 ft
400 ft
250 ft

3   6   9   12 miles

AT A GLANCE The Hidden World of Quabbin: Petersham and Dana

DISTANCE: 14 miles
ELEVATION GAIN: 918 feet
MODERATE

0.0   Start at Quabbin Access Gate 40, about 4 miles south of Petersham on Route 32A. Head southwest.

1.8   Arrive at Dana Common. Spend some time strolling around. Continue southwest on Dana Road.

3.7   Arrive viewpoint for the reservoir. Continue south.

3.8   Bend to the left uphill to cross a low ridge.

5.3   Arrive at fishing access point at Pottapaug Dam. After dam, continue east and then south on Hell Huddle Road.

7.0   Left on Greenwich Road.

7.4   Left on Mellon Road.

9.1   Continue straight on four-wheel-drive Mellon Road. (Alternatively, take a right on Breen Road and then a left on Route 32A.)

10.0   Left on Route 32A.

11.5   Right on Dana Road.

11.9   Left on Carter Pond Road.

12.3   Left on Woodward Road.

13.5   Right on 32A.

14.0   Arrive at Gate 40 parking.

24

Reformatory Branch and the Battle Road

Concord, Bedford, and Lexington, Massachusetts

DISTANCE: 15.9 miles
ELEVATION GAIN: 536 feet
EASY/MODERATE
An unusual sense of isolation and a way-back time travel road within the Boston metropolitan area.

It's an interesting challenge to find back-roads biking in the midst of urban and suburban sprawl. I was tickled when I devised this route, made up mostly of three very different bike trails. It allows you, at different points, to dislocate in time and space and feel transported, miles from urban hubbub and centuries from today.

Start this ride in the parking lot of the Millbrook Tarry, an upscale commercial development at the corner of Lowell and Keyes Roads, about a third of a mile north of downtown Concord. Plug Trail's End Cafe into your GPS to find the location and park just opposite the cafe. Head out Keyes Road, cross Lowell Road, and there's a small kiosk and a narrow path

snaking into the woods—The Reformatory Branch Rail Trail. It feels like a bit of a secret. The first tenth of a mile is single-track, not following the original railbed, but soon becomes double-track wide. This railbed was an extension from the Belmont Depot to the Concord Reformatory for about 50 years. Discontinued in 1962, it now provides a remarkably solitary walking and biking experience. The surface is packed dirt, fine for hybrid and gravel bikes, not so fine for road bikes. Muddy patches every now and again. This trail has not been improved like the upcoming trails.

For the first couple of miles, you're on the edge of the Great Meadows National Wildlife Refuge. Lots of opportunities to park your bike and stroll on the refuge trails. Very pretty in the fall with vibrant red maples around the edges. It's remarkable how isolated this stretch can seem. Yes, there are jets overhead and play structures in backyards, but more of the time, it's serene, abandoned farm meadows, oak and pine forests, jewelweed in the trailside ditches. Look for the yellow wooden flag on one of the granite posts which was a reminder to engineers to sound the whistle to alert traffic on an upcoming road. And then, after about 4 miles, you're in a suburban neighborhood followed by a school bus depot and, voilà, Bedford Depot.

The world now changes. At Bedford you join the Minuteman Commuter Bike Trail, which connects with the Boston MTA at Alewife Station in Cambridge. The Depot is often thronged with spandexed road bikers, families with little kids in trailers, recumbent bikers, riders of all sizes, shapes, and colors. It's a multicultural scene. Biker amenities abound. Shaded benches, restrooms, even a free sunscreen dispenser! Past the Depot, the trail is now wide, paved,

THE REFORMATORY BRANCH TRAIL SKIRTS THE EDGE OF THE BEAUTIFUL GREAT MEADOWS NATIONAL WILDLIFE REFUGE

even a bit crowded. Road crossings are well-engineered with lights and crossing lanes. The pace picks up and you feel compelled to put your head down and chew up those 4 miles to Lexington.

At Hancock Street, take a right off the bike trail and poof, you're at Lexington Green. Yes, *the* Lexington Green battleground where the first blood was spilled at the beginning of the Revolutionary War. Find the memorial stone with the famous quote from Captain John Parker, "Stand Your Ground. Don't fire unless fired upon. But if they mean to have a war, let it begin here." Who fired first? No one's really sure.

For the rest of the bike ride, you'll follow the route that the Redcoats traveled

to Concord and then retreated back along. Unless you want to cruise around in downtown Lexington, cruise down to the triangular tip of the green where the Minuteman statue stands and take a right on Massachusetts Avenue. This is definitely not a back road. But there's a well-defined shoulder, a bikeable sidewalk, bikes are allowed in the main lane, and you'll go up and over the only sizeable hill of the route. Nice cruise down the backside, and then you cross Route 128/95. Immediately, take a right on Wood Street, a left on Old Massachusetts Avenue, and then you'll see the granite post marking the entrance to the Battle Road Trail.

For the next 5 miles, you'll look for these granite posts at each intersection to stay on the Battle Road Trail. It's a remarkable accomplishment that the park service has managed to make this narrow corridor feel like long ago. The trail is as appropriately backroads-y as it might have been in 1775, not fruff-ified. It's sandy and gravelly, a bit gullied out in some places, lots of little ups and downs, massive oaks arching over the trail. Silly for me to provide any historical narrative because there are great interpretive panels all along the way, and authentically preserved houses that existed at the time. Stop in at the visitor center to see the quick theatrical portrayal of the events of that night—it's well done.

The only slightly confusing place along the trail is at the Bloody Angle, one of the bloodiest ambush sites for the Redcoats. It's a clearly defined, rock-walled bit of meadow. At the point of the triangle, take a left, then a right at the next corner of the triangle, and then the next left by the granite post. After this point you drop into a little hollow, traffic noise disappears, it's an April afternoon long ago, and if you listen carefully, you can hear musket fire and shouting voices in the distance.

From this point on, the riding gets more interesting. There are boardwalks across marshes, old farm fields, wild lettuce seed fluff floating across the trail. You'll feel like you've gotten to the end at roads or parking lots, but the trail continues until you get to Old Bedford Road. A quick left and then right onto Lexington Road. The rest of the ride is a bit of a rude awakening from your historical slumber. But there's a good shoulder and a bikeable sidewalk. And museums galore—Louisa May Alcott's Orchard House, the Concord Museum, the Ralph Waldo Emerson House. Bend around the Concord Green, passing the stately Colonial Inn, and take a right on Lowell Road. Millbrook Tarry is just up a bit on your left. It's amazing to realize that you just circumnavigated Hanscom Airforce Base and never realized it was there.

DINING OPPORTUNITIES

Trail's End Cafe is right here, it caters to bicyclists, it offers "carefully crafted comfort food," and it's open for lunch and dinner. There's very hip avocado toast, a wide array of healthy sandwiches and soups, a full service bar, and nice outdoor seating. Hard to get a table on pretty autumn afternoons, but worth checking out.

Concord Market, "an artisanal market," is like a miniature Whole Foods, pricey but appealing. My recommendation is that you do some picnic shopping here—some tuna salad, cut-up fruit, a

BEAUTIFULLY RESTORED 18TH-CENTURY HOMES LINE THE BATTLE ROAD TRAIL

TREASURE HUNT: HARD NOT TO FEEL CHILLS UP YOUR SPINE WHEN YOU FIND THIS MEMORIAL STONE

nice chunk of manchego, a baguette, and then locate one of the shaded picnic tables in the grassy park adjacent to the parking lot. A bit self-consciously chic perhaps, but a cozy way to end a bike ride.

SWIMMING OPPORTUNITY

Surprisingly, there is a good swim spot in the midst of suburban sprawl. In keeping with the historical theme of this ride, head over to the slender beach at **Walden Pond**. This 100-foot-deep kettle pond, nestled in dense woods, offers a refreshing plunge after a ride. Emulate Thoreau, who said, "Every morning was a cheerful invitation to make my life of equal simplicity, and I may say innocence, with Nature herself . . . I got up early and bathed in the pond; that was a religious exercise, and one of the best things which I did." It can get busy though; when the parking lot is full, you're turned away. You can call the state park to assess the parking situation.

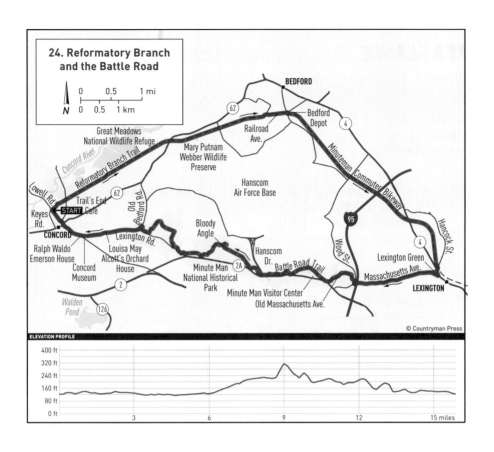

24. Reformatory Branch and the Battle Road

0   0.5   1 mi
0   0.5   1 km

BEDFORD

Great Meadows National Wildlife Refuge

Mary Putnam Webber Wildlife Preserve

Railroad Ave.

Bedford Depot

Minuteman Commuter Bikeway

Concord River

Reformatory Branch Trail

Lowell Rd.

Trail's End Cafe

START

Keyes Rd.

CONCORD

Ralph Waldo Emerson House

Concord Museum

Louisa May Alcott's Orchard House

Lexington Rd.

Old Bedford Rd.

Hanscom Air Force Base

Bloody Angle

Minute Man National Historical Park

Hanscom Dr.

Battle Road Trail

Wood St.

95

4

Lexington Green

Massachusetts Ave.

Hancock St.

LEXINGTON

Minute Man Visitor Center

Old Massachusetts Ave.

Walden Pond

126

2

© Countryman Press

ELEVATION PROFILE

400 ft
320 ft
240 ft
160 ft
80 ft
0 ft

3   6   9   12   15 miles

AT A GLANCE Reformatory Branch and the Battle Road: Concord, Bedford, and Lexington

DISTANCE: 15.9 miles
ELEVATION GAIN: 536 feet
EASY/MODERATE

0.0 Park in Millbrook Tarry lot near Trail's End Cafe. Start ride at intersection of Keyes and Lowell Roads, north of Concord Green on Reformatory Branch Trail. First 0.1 miles a bit of single track.

0.1 Continue straight ahead on double-track Reformatory Branch. Cruise past Great Meadows Refuge and Mary Putnam Webber Preserve.

3.9 Pop out on Railroad Street. Continue straight.

4.2 Arrive at Bedford Depot. Continue east and south toward Lexington on Minuteman Commuter Bikeway.

7.9 Turn right on Hancock Street. Explore Lexington Green ending at Minuteman statue.

8.0 Right on Massachusetts Avenue.

9.4 Right on Wood Street and quick left on Old Massachusetts Avenue.

9.5 Enter Battle Road Trail.

10.3 Optional turn into NPS Park Visitor Center.

12.0 At tip of Bloody Angle, bear left, then next right, then next left at post.

14.3 Left on Old Bedford Road and then quick right on Lexington Road.

15.6 Arrive at Concord Green and head around, past Colonial Inn and take a right on Lowell Street.

15.9 Arrive back at Trail's End Cafe.

25

Back Woods and Kettle Ponds
Wellfleet and Truro, Massachusetts

DISTANCE: 18.4 miles
ELEVATION GAIN: 760 feet
MODERATE

Discover the lost world of the kettle ponds, sand roads, scrub oak, and pine forests on the Outer Cape. A variety of paved and challenging sand/fire roads.

Everyone knows the Cape Cod Rail Trail that runs from Dennis to Wellfleet. There are numerous good loops that include this well-traveled trail. Ocean Drive in Wellfleet is also on the Greatest Hits list of New England biking. But, after 40 years of exploring the hidden lanes and less-traveled paved roads, I am going to introduce you to one of the great, mildly challenging, off-the-radar, Outer Cape loops. Not for road bikes. Mountain or hybrid bikes necessary—or at least something with fatter tires that won't sink in at the sand traps along the way.

Look at the maps of Cape Cod National Seashore and you'll see that there's only one place, in Wellfleet and Truro, where the park stretches all the way from ocean to bay. This ride rambles you through this widest section of the park, away from the crowded beaches and fried clam outlets on Route 6. Be prepared to feel a bit lost

EVEN THE STARTING POINT AT MAYO BEACH PARKING LOT IS PHOTOGENIC

SECRET SINGLE TRACK ON THE ABANDONED RAILBED
BETWEEN RYDER BEACH ROAD AND PAMET POINT ROAD

town beach. (There are 17 of these scattered throughout these woods—many offer idyllic swimming.) Store for future reference.

Just past the pond take a left on Eldredge Road, your first foray onto sand roads. Unclip or take your feet out of the cages if you're not used to sand-road riding. You'll be needing to put your feet down quickly. You're immediately in the hush of the pine forests with perhaps an audible hint of distant surf. No homes, no cars, maybe a fox. At the bottom of a dip, you'll encounter your first sand trap—deep and soft and difficult to negotiate. At a prominent V intersection, bear left on what is called Way 632 (no sign). Skirt the puddles, go straight ahead at the next four corners, and you're back to pavement to take a right on Gross Hill Road. Gull Pond is visible through the trees down to your left. Up a bit of a hill, left downhill on Ocean Drive, and then a quick left on Thoreau Way. You'll recognize the entrance because of the 20 or so name signs on the tree. (If you'd like, take a quick detour down to popular Newcomb Hollow ocean beach, just a quarter-mile past Thoreau Way.)

On Thoreau Way, look ahead and assess which side of the lane has firmer sand—it'll switch back and forth. Your other challenge is to not get lost. It's hard to differentiate between Thoreau Way, side lanes, and driveways. Essentially, stay on the most traveled byway. Cottages hide back amidst the pines. You're in the mysterious Back Woods. If you encounter a car, it's so narrow you'll have to stop and pull your bike off the side of the road. At the prominently signed intersection of Thoreau and Black Pond Roads, you're going to take a left. (Psst! I'll let you in on a secret. Take a right here, bear right at the Slough Pond Road intersection, and you'll soon come

and for only a few ocean views. This is more of an intimate, interior ride.

Park in the town parking lot at Mayo Beach on Kendrick Avenue in Wellfleet, just west of the town wharf. Turn right out of the parking lot, pass the wharf, and head north on Commercial Street. You'll pass Mac's Shack, the lumber yard, and a number of art galleries. Don't turn up Bank Street into the village but bear right to stay on Commercial. At Main Street hitch a right and then a quick left on Long Pond Road. You'll cross above busy Route 6, barely realizing it's there, and you'll soon cross the park boundary into the world of the kettle ponds. Long Pond will be on your right—one of the easily accessible ponds with a pretty

to one of the best pond swim spots in the Back Woods—Horseleech Pond. Oddly named because there are zero leeches. Caribbean clear, sandy, freshwater a stone's throw from the ocean. Priceless.)

Back at the Black Pond intersection, turn left. It's 1.5 miles out to Route 6 on sandy lanes. You'll pass Williams, Slough, and Herring Ponds on the way. Try to stay on the best-traveled track in the lane. Don't take lefts or rights. At dreaded Route 6, take a right for 0.3 miles, take a right on Rose Road, and then take another quick right on Collins Road. Serenity returns. You're in Truro now. You'll pass a pullover for another great swim spot on Great Pond and then climb to the top of a rise. (There's a chained-off Fire Road to the right with access to a labyrinth of cool trails. Next book.) For now, swoop pleasantly downhill on smooth pavement and take a left on South Pamet Road Pass under dreaded Route 6, and stop for a cold drink at Jams in one of the lost villages of Truro. (Truro doesn't really have a bustling village center like Wellfleet, rather three or four sort-of villages scattered about.) From Jams, go right on Center Road and then right on Depot Road and stay on it all the way out to Pamet Harbor. Quiet boat scene, great sunsets, and views of distant beaches. Head back up Depot and take a right on Mill Pond Road to pass through marshes in the process of being converted from freshwater back to saltwater. Right on Old County Road for a climb and then heathy hills on your left. You'll have to interrupt your downhill swoop to take a fast right onto Ryder Beach Road.

Now for your next Back Woods challenge. Opposite Quanset Road, take a left on what is marked as Diana's Trail. It's really an unimproved section of the Cape Cod rail trail to Provincetown. The first quarter-mile will test your sand riding

skills. Then it'll narrow to a firmer single track with wonderful marsh views and then a secretive tunnel requiring some brush dodging. It's only 1.2 miles, but it will seem much longer and it'll feel like your own private Cape Cod.

You'll pop out on Pamet Point Road and take a right on Bound Brook Island Road heading south (don't go uphill on Bound Brook Road here), meandering along the marshes of the Herring River. Still serenely quiet except for kingfishers, redwing blackbirds, and herons. At the intersection with Coles Neck Road, stay right on what is now Pole Dike Road, and then soon a right on High Toss

TREASURE HUNT: THE BIKE WON'T BE THERE, BUT FIND THIS ACCESS TRAIL DOWN TO THIS TINY SECRET BEACH ON HORSELEECH POND

IT'S ALMOST ALWAYS SERENE AT PAMET HARBOR AT SUNSET

Road, a wide, well-packed gravel road for about a half-mile until Snake Creek Road bends off to the left. Here, stay straight on High Toss Road through Herring River marshes. This is your last off-road challenge. This next 0.2 miles begins the roller coaster section of the ride and may be littered with big, deep-ish puddles that you might have to walk around. Once you cross the actual Herring River, you'll take a left on an unnamed fire road. I love this stretch that rolls along between the back side of Griffin Island and the marshes. Pristine isolation and pleasantly challenging biking. When you make it to the pavement at Chequessett Neck Road, congratulations! You've earned your Sand Roads Biking Badge. And be sure to check for ticks.

Take a left on Chequessett Neck. Long views across to Great Island and Wellfleet Bay. You can relax with stable asphalt under your tires, but there are three 50-foot hills along the way before you cruise past all the cute, shingled cottages and arrive back at Mayo Beach.

DINING OPPORTUNITIES

Really, there's no better beachside clam shack on the Cape than **Mac's on the Pier**, right around the corner. We make a pilgrimage here every spring and fall. Jen gets a Fried Oyster Po'boy with a side of slaw, and I get a Grilled Swordfish sandwich. There's great chowder, Portuguese kale soup or try the unusually delicious Crunch Bowls. Umbrella-ed tables and a sheltered outdoor seating area for when there's a wind-driven shower off the bay.

Other great dining in Wellfleet—the classy upstairs bar at **Winslow's Tavern** and the outside patio or the bar for watching Red Sox games at the **Wicked Oyster**. A beer and some fried shrimp at the **Bookstore**, right across from Mayo Beach, particularly at sunset, is cool too.

SWIMMING OPPORTUNITIES

For an exploratory experience, make your way down very sandy lanes to **Bound Brook Island Beach** in Wellfleet. You passed the turn right at the end of the railbed. There's enough space to park about three cars and then there's a bit of a tromp out to this bay beach. You'll have it to yourself.

The truly great finds are the kettle hole ponds. The water is Caribbean clear, the bottoms are soft and sandy, and the temperature is much warmer than the ocean or the bay. You passed the Wellfleet town beach on **Long Pond** and I foolishly let you in on the secret of **Horseleech Pond**. If you're a true seeker, find your way to the tiny beaches at the **Sluiceway between Gull and Higgins Ponds**. Again, very few parking spaces, lots of poison ivy to avoid, but ultimately charming and unlike any other beaches you'll find on the Cape.

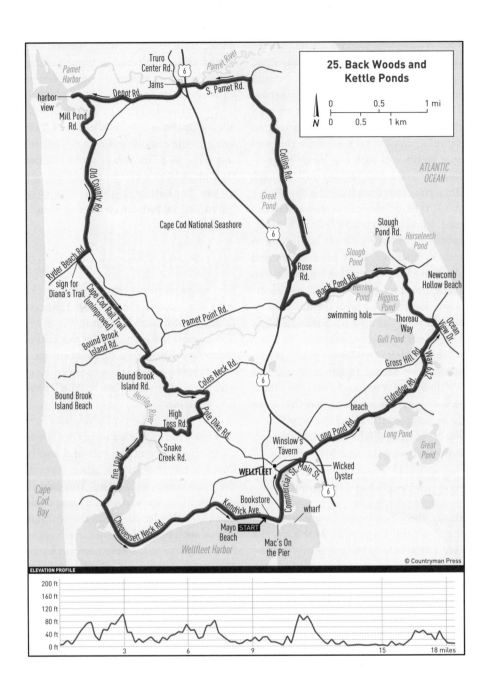

25. Back Woods and Kettle Ponds

Pamet Harbor

Truro Center Rd.

Pamet River

harbor view

Depot Rd.

Jams

S. Pamet Rd.

Mill Pond Rd.

Old County Rd.

Collins Rd.

Great Pond

Cape Cod National Seashore

ATLANTIC OCEAN

Slough Pond Rd.

Horseleech Pond

Slough Pond

Newcomb Hollow Beach

Ryder Beach Rd.

sign for Diana's Trail

Cape Cod Rail Trail (unimproved)

Rose Rd.

Black Pond Rd.

Herring Pond

Higgins Pond

swimming hole

Thoreau Way

Gull Pond

Bound Brook Island Rd.

Pamet Point Rd.

Gross Hill Rd.

Ocean View Dr.

Way 6-32

Bound Brook Island Rd.

Coles Neck Rd.

Eldredge Rd.

Bound Brook Island Beach

Herring River

High Toss Rd.

Pole Dike Rd.

beach

Long Pond Rd.

Long Pond

Great Pond

Snake Creek Rd.

fire road

Winslow's Tavern

WELLFLEET

Wicked Oyster

Cape Cod Bay

Chequessett Neck Rd.

Bookstore

Kendrick Ave.

Commercial St.

Main St.

wharf

Mayo Beach

START

Mac's On the Pier

Wellfleet Harbor

© Countryman Press

ELEVATION PROFILE

200 ft
160 ft
120 ft
80 ft
40 ft
0 ft

3   6   9   15   18 miles

AT A GLANCE Back Woods and Kettle Ponds: Wellfleet and Truro

DISTANCE: 18.4 miles
ELEVATION GAIN: 760 feet
MODERATE

0.0 Park in Wellfleet town parking lot at Mayo Beach on Kendrick Avenue. Turn right on Kendrick Avenue and then bend left around onto Commercial Street.

0.8 Right on Main Street. Quick left onto Long Pond Road. Pass Long Pond.

1.9 Left on Eldredge Road—a sand/fire road.

2.4 Bear left at V intersection on Way 632 and then stay straight ahead at next four-way sand–road intersection.

2.7 Right on Gross Hill Road.

3.0 Left on Ocean Drive and then quick left on Thoreau Way.

3.8 Left on Black Pond Road.

5.2 Right on Route 6.

5.5 Right on Rose Road and then a right on paved Collins Road.

7.8 Left on South Pamet Road, and once under Route 6 bear right to . . .

8.6 Arrive lost village of Truro Center and Jams. From Jams parking lot, right on Truro Center Road and a quick right on Depot Road. Follow Depot Road to end to . . .

10.0 Arrive at Pamet Harbor. Retrace steps on Depot Road and . . .

10.1 Right on Mill Pond Road.

10.7 Right on Old County Road.

11.8 Right on Ryder Beach Road and then quick left on Diana's Trail/old railbed.

13.2 Right on Bound Brook Island Road. (Don't go uphill to right, stay flat and straight ahead.)

14.1 At Coles Neck Road bear right on what is now Pole Dike Road.

14.4 Right and then bear right again on High Toss Road.

15.1 When Snake Creek goes left, stay straight on High Toss. Big puddles.

15.3 Left on unnamed fire road.

16.2 Left on Chequessett Neck Road.

18.4 Arrive at Mayo Beach parking.

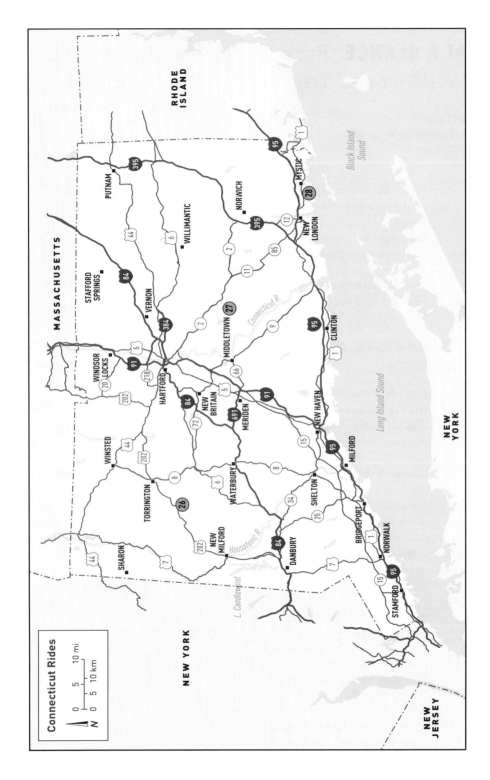

Connecticut Rides

N

0 — 5 — 10 mi
0 — 5 — 10 km

MASSACHUSETTS

RHODE ISLAND

NEW YORK

NEW JERSEY

NEW YORK

Block Island Sound

Long Island Sound

PUTNAM

WILLIMANTIC

NORWICH

MYSTIC

NEW LONDON

STAFFORD SPRINGS

VERNON

MIDDLETOWN

Connecticut R.

CLINTON

WINDSOR LOCKS

HARTFORD

NEW BRITAIN

MERIDEN

NEW HAVEN

MILFORD

WINSTED

TORRINGTON

WATERBURY

SHELTON

BRIDGEPORT

SHARON

NEW MILFORD

Housatonic R.

DANBURY

NORWALK

STAMFORD

L. Candlewood

RIGHT: MYSTIC LIGHTHOUSE IN MYSTIC, CT

CONNECTICUT RIDES

RIDES

(West to East)

YOUR RIDE STARTS ALONG THIS BEAUTIFUL SECTION OF MARSH ON THE GREENWAY TRAIL

26

White Memorial Foundation
Litchfield and Bantam Lake, Connecticut

DISTANCE: 12.3 miles
ELEVATION GAIN: 744 feet
MODERATE
A wonderful ride with some sections that are magical. A unique bike experience. Worth the drive to explore this area in depth.

It's hard not to like Litchfield, Connecticut. As you rise up from the valley into the Litchfield Hills, the temperature goes down five or more degrees. The village is perched on a hilltop with a small green, appealing cafes, and many shops. Just south of the village, White Memorial Foundation protects 4,000 acres and is dedicated to instilling understanding, appreciation, and respect for the natural world. It's the reason for this ride. The facilities and trail network make it feel like a private, well-tended state park without the crowds. This ride exemplifies diverse textures—woods roads, marsh paths, quiet backroads, a bit of busy highway, bridges, winding along rivers, and a

bit of complicated way-finding. It's a true treasure. Make sure you have a copy of the White Memorial Foundation map, on paper or downloaded on your phone, for navigation during some parts of this ride.

Start this ride south of Litchfield on Whites Woods Road, where there's clearly marked Bike Trail crossing signage and stripes on the road. On the White Memorial Foundation (WMF) map, it's the Greenway Trail, (G). Park in an asphalt area right before the trail—be sure not to block the gate at the upper end. Head south along the Greenway trail through expansive marshlands and then through spaciously towering pines. Stay straight as the G trail becomes Mattatuck (M) and you're soon at paved Bissell Road. Go straight across onto Whitehall Road, a gravel road that's part of the nature center complex. You're along the scenically marshy and windy Bantam River for a while and then you'll take a right to stay on Whitehall Road (I, Interpretive Trail on WMF map) up through meadows, past the old White mansion which houses the nature museum, and into the main parking lot.

Now find your way onto the Lake Trail (L) marked with yellow rectangles. (Though many of these are called trails, they're really double-track, well-maintained woods roads providing a mildly challenging but intimate experience.) Pretty soon the L trail forks, and your temptation is to go left downhill and toward the lake. Instead, head uphill for a short climb over the ridge of Windmill Hill and then down, across a marshy stream, and eventually come out on the road to the Litchfield Town Beach. If you get lost in this section, you might wind up on rooty and marshy footpaths down by the lake that you have to walk on. Just keep going and bearing left and you'll wind up on the beach road.

HIPPOS AND TIGERS LURK JUST AROUND THE BEND ON THE MARSHY MATTATUCK TRAIL

Road to assess it for a mid-ride or post-ride swim. Cars need stickers but if you arrive by bike, you're cool. Continue north on East Shore Road—very different from earlier Bantam Lake Road. The east side is where the swells live. There are big gated estates with manicured lawns sprawling down to the shore. And, while the other shore road was flat, this is very up and down—three 75- to 100-foot climbs along this stretch.

At the end of East Shore, take a left on Alain White/Mattatuck Road, descend a bit and look for a gravel parking pull-off on the right at the entrance to the gated Beaver Pond (B) trail. Now the fun begins. You'll be on WMF trails for the rest of the ride. They're easier to follow now, but keep your map at the ready—lots of options and turns. This part of the ride is, and I don't use this word lightly, magical. It sounds complicated, but it's way worth it. The trails are gravelly, sometimes a bit challenging, but always well-maintained. Here we go.

On Beaver Pond (B), take the second right onto Little Cathedral (LC). This is a beautiful, isolated trail that takes you up one side of a little stream valley and

Take a right on the beach road and then take a left on North Shore Road. From the mosquitoed hinterlands, you've now arrived in summer vacationland. Follow North Shore Road for a mile and then take a left on Bantam Lake Road. Cottages, motorboats, jet skis, water-skiers, tasteful convenience stores, and a bit of traffic abound. It's a pleasant ramble. At the end of Bantam Lake, climb a bit and then turn left on Route 109 and climb some more. This is the only busy state highway section of the ride, but it's a good counterpoint to what's coming. You'll pass Camp Columbia State Park on the right, a good alternative starting point for this ride.

Take a left on East Shore Road, leaving the traffic behind. At the bottom of the hill turn into the Morris Town Beach

TREASURE HUNT: FIND THIS SIGN SOMEWHERE ALONG THE BANTAM RIVER

then down the other side. Almost at the end of LC, take a right on Big Cathedral (BC), then drop down (cool downhill), cross Beaver Pond (B), and soon you'll be on Mattatuck (M) for the rest of the ride.

At the fork in the trail, bear left (M) to head over toward Cranberry Pond. The trail flattens out and you emerge out of the forest into African marsh savannah land, with reed canary grass and cattails towering above you. You can feel the hippos and tigers lurking back in the impenetrable vegetation. Out of Africa, back to Connecticut, you continue north on Mattatuck (M), crossing Webster Road into Catlin Woods. You pleasantly twist and turn, ignoring trail options that diverge off to the right and left, following the blue rectangles. Cross Whites Woods Road, bending a little to the right into a gravel parking area by the river. Find where

Mattatuck bends out of the parking area along the Bantam River and pause on the bike bridge across the river to watch kayakers and sometimes kids jumping off the bridge. Just past the bridge, you're back at Whitehall Road. Take a right, cross Bissell Road, and follow the trail back the way you started under the lofty pines, across the marsh bridge, and back to your car.

DINING OPPORTUNITY

There are three or four nice little cafes on the green in Litchfield. We highly recommend the **Market Place Tavern** located in the Old Litchfield Prison. Indoor and outdoor seating, beautiful restoration, interesting menu. The website says, "The Tavern which overlooks the Litchfield Green, is the oldest public building in

CROSSING THE BANTAM RIVER TOWARD THE END OF THE RIDE

town and one of the oldest penal facilities in the state. It was built in 1812 to serve as a jail for British prisoners during the War of 1812. A cell block and a three-story wing with additional cell blocks, which now is part of the restaurant's bar area, was added in 1846." Now restored and converted to commercial use, the interior was designed to preserve the history of the building. There's a nice mix of brick, barn wood, cast iron, and comfortable leather booths

For a post-ride quaff, there's an unusual selection of craft brews. I recommend the Thomas Hooker Tropical Ale, a cross between an IPA and a piña colada. Sounds weird, but it's delicious. And we had a Sweet and Spicy Crispy Chicken bowl that was distinctively different and healthy. Worthy of repeat visits.

SWIMMING OPPORTUNITIES

The town beaches in Connecticut have a somewhat different vibe than in New Hampshire and Vermont. Here, there's more of an enforced residents–only vibe. But if you arrive on bike or foot, no one will notice you.

You passed the **Litchfield Town Beach** earlier. Nice place to swim. You can probably find a place to park out on North Shore Road, or if it's a quiet mid-week day, you can decide what to do. Same is true for the **Morris Town Beach** that you passed earlier on East Shore Road. Big meadows, restrooms, probably unstaffed much of the time.

There's also **Sandy Beach** in Morris off East Shore Road—*"the best kept secret on Bantam Lake"*—that's open to non-residents with an admission fee. Big wide beach, a float with a slide, restrooms, a concession stand, the whole nine yards.

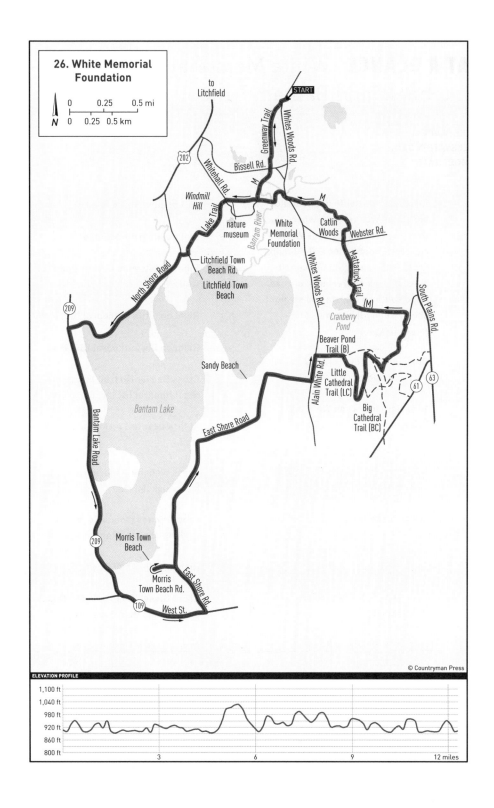

26. White Memorial
Foundation

0   0.25   0.5 mi

N   0   0.25   0.5 km

to
Litchfield

START

Greenway Trail

Whites Woods Rd.

Bissell Rd.

202

Whitehall Rd.

M

M

Windmill
Hill

Lake Trail

Bantam River

nature
museum

White
Memorial
Foundation

Catlin
Woods

Webster Rd.

Mattatuck Trail

Litchfield Town
Beach Rd.

Litchfield Town
Beach

North Shore Road

Whites Woods Rd.

Cranberry
Pond

(M)

South Plains Rd.

209

Beaver Pond
Trail (B)

Sandy Beach

Alain White Rd.

Little
Cathedral
Trail (LC)

61   63

Bantam Lake

Bantam Lake Road

East Shore Road

Big
Cathedral
Trail (BC)

209

Morris Town
Beach

East Shore Rd.

Morris
Town Beach Rd.

109   West St.

© Countryman Press

ELEVATION PROFILE

1,100 ft
1,040 ft
980 ft
920 ft
860 ft
800 ft

3   6   9   12 miles

AT A GLANCE White Memorial Foundation: Litchfield and Bantam Lake

DISTANCE: 12.3 miles
ELEVATION GAIN: 744 feet
MODERATE

0.0	Start this ride south of Litchfield on Whites Woods Road, where the Greenway (G) Trail, on the White Memorial Foundation (WMF) map, crosses the road. Small asphalt place to park on west side of road. Head south on (G), staying straight ahead when (G) becomes Mattatuck (M).
0.5	Cross Bissell Road onto Whitehall Road/Mattatuck (M).
0.8	Turn right to stay on Whitehall Road, now Interpretive Trail (I).
1.0	Pass WMF parking area staying on Whitehall Road and look for beginning of Lake Trail (L) on your left.
1.1	Left on Lake Trail.
1.2	Bear right uphill to stay on Lake Trail.
1.7	Turn right on Litchfield Town Beach Road.
1.8	Left on North Shore Road.
2.9	Left on Route 209/Bantam Lake Road.
4.9	Left on Route 109. Uphill with traffic.

5.6	Left on East Shore Road.
8.1	Left on Alain White Road.
8.2	Right at gate onto Beaver Pond (B) trail.
8.4	Right on Little Cathedral (LC) trail.
9.1	Right on Big Cathedral (BC) trail.
9.4	Cross Beaver (B) trail to stay on Big Cathedral (BC) trail.
9.6	At fork bear left on Mattatuck (M) trail.
10.5	Cross Webster Road and stay on Mattatuck (M) trail.
11.3	Cross Whites Woods Road into parking area and continue on M.
11.5	Right on Whitehall Road.
11.8	Cross Bissell Road onto Mattatuck (M) trail and then Greenway (G).
12.3	Arrive back at parking area.

High and Low
The Air Line and East Hampton, Connecticut

DISTANCE: 15.1 miles
ELEVATION GAIN: 1099 feet
MODERATE/CHALLENGING

A surprisingly beautiful ride in a quiet corner of eastern Connecticut. The stretch along River Road is heavenly.

The Air Line is a 19th-century railbed in the New York-to-Boston corridor that was transformed into a bike trail over the past couple of decades. The name comes from the high bridges and viaducts crossing the many steep-sided river valleys along the way. The stretch on this ride includes some of those high places, though the really high viaduct has been replaced with fill. Cool nonetheless.

Park for this ride where the Air Line crosses CT Route 149, in the northwestern part of Colchester, Connecticut. There's a large, well-defined, and well-used parking lot here. Head west on the trail. You'll likely have the company of dog-walkers, electric bikers, and

UP HIGH ON WHAT USED TO BE THE LATHAM VIADUCT

chatting fitness groups—very convivial. The ride gets quickly scenic as you pass a pretty marsh on the upper stretches of the Jeremy River. After a road crossing at grade, it's pretty wild and slightly uphill for the next 5 miles. In October, with the foliage changing, the trail is a tunnel of golden light encouraging you onward. Just past mile 3 you'll cross Dickinson Creek on what used to be the Latham Viaduct—great views of the rolling hills to the south.

As you approach East Hampton, you'll come to a pond on Cattle Lot Brook and then exit the trail, taking a right on Smith Street and then a left on Flanders Road. This allows you to slide into the downtown of East Hampton, somewhat of a lost village because it was once known as Belltown, the capital of bell fabrication in the country. There were 30 bell foundries here in the 19th and early 20th centuries and now only one remains. Hard to imagine, but some of the old mills give you a sense of what this town must have felt like. Cruise down Summit Street into town and stop to appreciate the unusually narrow and sky-piercing spire on the Congregational Church, then turn left on Main Street, but only for a moment. Look carefully on the left for a small parking lot and the entrance to the Air Line Trail heading back to the east, up a short steep and then twisty section to get you headed back into the woods.

Back at Smith Street, you'll turn right for a climb past an elementary school and come to Route 16, the busy highway section of the ride. Remember all that elevation you gained on the Air Line? You're expending it now. Mid downhill, after about 0.75 miles you'll turn left on

THE TRAIL SKIRTS THE EDGE OF DAYBREAK POND

Flatbrook Road to get you away from traffic. It's a lot of up-and-down, but really pretty. Rejoining Route 16, it's another swoop down to a left on Comstock Bridge Road at one of the few covered bridges left in Connecticut.

Check out the covered bridge and then enter into Salmon River State Forest. Electric lines and telephone poles disappear, and you're slotted into a steep valley along the gamboling river. It'll change your attitude about Connecticut. (Note the numerous, easily accessible swimming holes along here. There's even a handicapped accessible fly fishing area that is off limits for swimming, but it sure looks like an attractive place to slip into the water.) Eventually you'll turn away from the river, pass under the Air Line through an impressively crafted stone archway, and continue along River Road through meadows and forest. When you reach the Air Line at grade again, take a left and you're back at your car in a couple of minutes. Even though the whole route back parallels the Air Line much of the way, it feels completely different.

TREASURE HUNT: A GRAND BUILDING FOR A CYCLE SHOP

DINING OPPORTUNITIES

These two options are both located right downtown near the end of the Air Line trail.

The **ECO Coffee House** would be a great stop for a mid-ride caffeine boost. And the sandwiches look amazing: "warm burrata sandwiched between salty prosciutto and arugula on a toasted French roll slathered with Pumpkin butter and a fig balsamic glaze." They claim to have the best avocado toast on the planet.

Po's Rice and Spice has a hip Asian menu and diners consider this the best Chinese and Thai food in the area. I'd love to try the Macadamia Fried Rice with shrimp, peapods, and pineapple.

SWIMMING OPPORTUNITIES

Salmon River State Forest. Not much to add here. There are at least a half dozen hemlock-shaded and sun-dappled places to get in the water along the Salmon River. Some have little sandy beaches. Most are easily accessible. Take your pick.

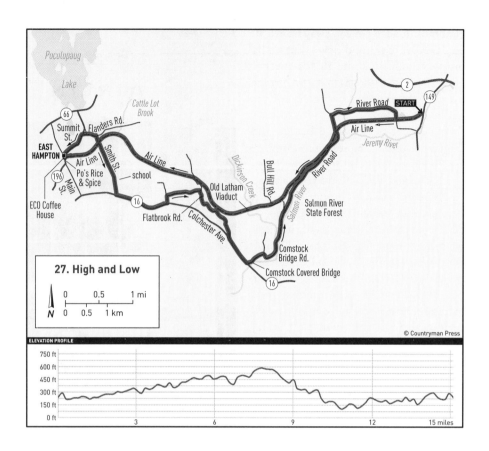

Pocotopaug
Lake

Cattle Lot
Brook

66

Summit
St.

Flanders Rd.

EAST
HAMPTON

Air Line

Smith St.

Air Line

196

Po's Rice
& Spice

Main St.

school

ECO Coffee
House

16

Flatbrook Rd.

Colchester Ave.

Old Latham
Viaduct

Dickinson Creek

Bull Hill Rd.

Salmon River

River Road

Salmon River
State Forest

Comstock
Bridge Rd.

Comstock Covered Bridge

16

River Road START

2

149

Air Line

Jeremy River

27. High and Low

N

| 0 | 0.5 | 1 mi |
| 0 | 0.5 | 1 km |

© Countryman Press

ELEVATION PROFILE

| 750 ft |
| 600 ft |
| 450 ft |
| 300 ft |
| 150 ft |
| 0 ft |

3   6   9   12   15 miles

AT A GLANCE High and Low: The Air Line and East Hampton

DISTANCE: 15.1 miles
ELEVATION GAIN: 1099 feet
MODERATE/CHALLENGING

0.0 — Park at the Air Line parking area where the trail crosses CT Route 149 in northwest Colchester, CT. Head west on trail.

3.2 — Old viaduct crossing over Dickenson Creek.

5.9 — Right off of trail onto Smith Street, then quick left onto Flanders Road.

6.2 — Left on Summit Street to cruise into East Hampton.

6.6 — Left on Main Street and then an immediate left on Air Line trail.

7.3 — Right off of trail onto Smith Street.

8.1 — Left on Route 16/Colchester Avenue.

8.9 — Left on Flatbrook Road. Turn right at next two junctions to stay on Flatbrook Road.

10.4 — Left on Route 16/Colchester Avenue.

10.8 — Left on Comstock Bridge Road.

11.9 — At junction with Bull Hill Road, bear right on River Road. Cross under Air Line at about 13.4 miles.

13.6 — Bear right to stay on River Road.

14.7 — Turn left to rejoin the Air Line.

15.1 — Arrive back at the Air Line parking area.

28

Oh, the Places You'll Go
Mystic and Bluff Point, Connecticut

DISTANCE: 17.2 miles
ELEVATION GAIN: 782 feet
MODERATE

A smorgasbord of seashore Connecticut, from touristy downtown to suburban neighborhoods to almost coastal wilderness to an unexpected village. Hybrid or mountain bikes required for part of the Bluff Point section of the ride.

This ride epitomizes "textural diversity." From touristy downtown to an abandoned trolley line to pretty beaches to the Amtrak corridor—the scenery and road surfaces are always changing. Find a place to park in downtown Mystic—Steamboat Wharf and the Amtrak Station are two options. In any case, the directions start from the drawbridge in the center of town, so you can see the massive bridge counterweights that hang over Main Street. Quite a sight.

From the bridge, tootle through the traffic west on Main Street and turn left on Water Street/Route 215/Elm Street for a not very scenic and somewhat traffic-y couple of miles to a turn on Brook Street. (Note an alternative starting point for

this ride at a small pull-off for Beebe Pond Park at around 2 miles, if you want to skip this out-and-back section.) On Brook Street you'll be disabused of the illusion that coastal biking is flat as you climb up and over a 100-foot hill. Cross Groton Long Point Road, stay on Brook, and then take a left on Haley Farm Lane to the parking area at Haley Farm State Park. Now the fun begins. Follow the gravel main lane through this wonderful overgrown farm of meadows and forest—a wonderful transition from suburbia to lost world. At 3.5 miles, you'll turn right on an oddly paved path that bends around and follows the path of an abandoned trolley line, straight as an arrow.

When suburbia appears, turn right on Knoxville Court, left on Midway Oval, and continue straight onto Fitch Avenue and then right on Depot Road until you take a left on Route 1.

Staying on the left side of Route 1 and just before crossing the river, turn left on the Poquonock River Boardwalk—a beautiful, immersive experience amidst the phragmites reeds. You're supposed to walk your bikes, so if you encounter pedestrians, be considerate. You'll pop out in a town park and playground and then take a right on Depot Street, cross under the Amtrak lines, and soon arrive at the parking area for Bluff Point Street Park.

Pass the gate and follow the main trail toward the point. Nice packed surface, a bit flooded at high tides, with expansive views out across the river to the barrier beach. Right before you get to the point, there's access to a shell beach on the right. Perfect place for a mid-ride swim in the warm waters of Long Island Sound.

For the next couple of miles, the surface can be dicey—chunky stone, bits of ledge—you don't want to be on a road bike here. But the sense of isolated

A VERY COOL WINDING BOARDWALK (BUT IF THERE ARE PEDESTRIANS, YOU SHOULD WALK)

A MOMENT OF RELAXATION BEFORE TAKING THE PLUNGE

straight ahead on an amiable section of single-track underneath the power lines down to where you can take a right onto Sunrise Road back into suburbia.

Now pay attention to this maze of directions. Left on Neptune, left on Nautilus, straight ahead on Anchorage Circle, bear left onto Bass Drive, left on Colony Road, and right on Mumford Cove Road, which becomes Groton Long Point Road. After passing pretty Esker Point Beach, take a right on Marsh Road to wend your way past Ford's Black and Blue (great local seafood) and Spicer's Marina (really big boats) and arrive in Noank, a perfect little lost coastal village, a bit reminiscent of Oak Bluffs on Martha's Vineyard. This is the freeform part of the ride. Take as much time as you want to knock around these pretty neighborhoods. Head out to Morgan Point, find the Historical Society, Noank Oyster, and the Latham Chester store. Eventually make your way to where the Mosher Avenue bridge cuts off of Ward Avenue over the Amtrak line to a right on Route 215/Elm Street. From here it's a straight shot north back to Mystic. Think of all the places you've been in the past 2 hours.

forest bliss with the ocean so nearby is wonderful. The last half-mile is a speedy but bumpy downhill back to the parking area.

From the parking area, take an unmarked gravel road to the right, bend to the left, and then back to the right. Eventually you'll wind up along the fence between you and the Amtrak corridor with the drama of fast trains zooming by. You'll wind up at a fenced-off suburban neighborhood at Neptune Drive. You can clamber over the fence or just stay

DINING OPPORTUNITIES

Ford's Black and Blue is a classic steak and seafood restaurant and it's casual enough to get lunch in your bike togs. We had the perfect mid-ride fried oyster lunch special there one beautiful April afternoon. Other innovative seafood dishes as well.

Back in Mystic, I recommend **Grass and Bone** on the east side of the river, just beyond the Whaler's Inn. It's a butcher shop with a great takeout or dine-outside menu. I had a unique Tijuana Chicken Caesar sandwich that

TREASURE HUNT: IT'S RARE TO FIND A BEACH WITH SO MANY SLIPPER SHELLS

was unlike anything I had ever tasted before. The noodle bowls, rotisserie chicken, and salads are sumptuous. Can't go wrong here.

SWIMMING OPPORTUNITIES

That beach at **Bluff Point State Park** is hard to beat. It's at the perfect point in the ride, very few people swim there because it's too far to walk, and much of the surface is slipper shells. We swam here in late October recently at high tide. The water was warm and calm, the beach was empty and there was a little raft of migrating ducks paddling around. It was close to blissful.

Esker Point Beach is another option. Easy to drive back to, a more conventional strand of white sand, right near Ford's Black and Blue and Noank. Worth checking out.

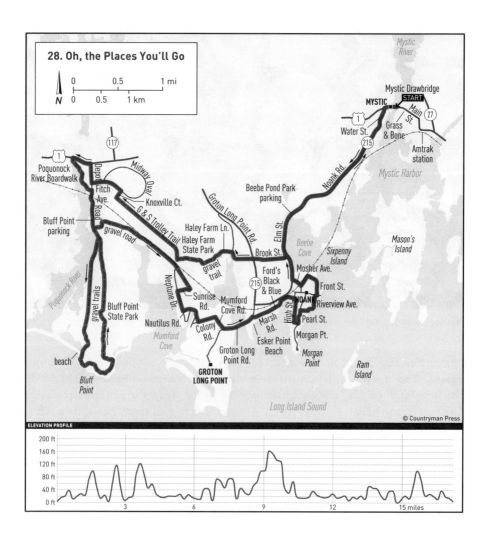

28. Oh, the Places You'll Go

N

| 0 | 0.5 | 1 mi |
| 0 | 0.5 | 1 km |

Mystic River

Mystic Drawbridge
START
MYSTIC
Main St.
27
Water St.
1
215
Grass & Bone
Amtrak station
117
Mystic Harbor
Poquonock River Boardwalk
1
Depot Rd.
Midway Oval
Noank Rd.
Beebe Pond Park parking
Fitch Ave.
Knoxville Ct.
G & S Trolley Trail
Groton Long Point Rd.
Elm St.
Bluff Point parking
Haley Farm Ln.
Haley Farm State Park
gravel road
Mason's Island
gravel trail
Brook St.
Beebe Cove
Sixpenny Island
Poquonock River
Neptune Dr.
215
Ford's Black & Blue
Mosher Ave.
Front St.
Sunrise Rd.
Mumford Cove Rd.
NOANK
Riverview Ave.
gravel trails
Bluff Point State Park
Nautilus Rd.
Colony Rd.
Marsh Rd.
High St.
Pearl St.
Morgan Pt.
Mumford Cove
Esker Point Beach
Morgan Point
beach
Groton Long Point Rd.
Ram Island
Bluff Point
GROTON LONG POINT
Long Island Sound

© Countryman Press

ELEVATION PROFILE

| 200 ft |
| 160 ft |
| 120 ft |
| 80 ft |
| 40 ft |
| 0 ft |

3   6   9   12   15 miles

AT A GLANCE Oh, the Places You'll Go: Mystic and Bluff Point

DISTANCE: 17.2 miles
ELEVATION GAIN: 782 feet
MODERATE

0.0 — Park somewhere in Mystic and get yourself to Bascule Drawbridge in the center of town. Head west on Main Street and then turn south on Water Street/Route 215/ which becomes Noank Road and then Elm Street.

2.2 — Right on Brook Street. Cross Groton Long Point Road.

2.9 — Left on Haley Farm Lane. Arrive state park lot and continue on main gravel road through Haley Farm State Park.

3.6 — Right on old G & S Trolley Trail.

4.5 — Right on Knoxville, left on Midway Oval, straight onto Fitch, right on Depot Road.

5.2 — Left on Route 1. Stay on left and look for. . . .

5.4 — Left on Poquonock Bridge Boardwalk. Walk if you encounter pedestrians.

5.9 — Right on Depot Road. Under Amtrak tracks. Arrive at Bluff Point parking.

6.3 — Pass around gate onto trail to Bluff Point.

7.8 — Arrive Bluff Point beach. Great swim spot. Continue on Bluff Point loop trail and be prepared for a stony ride.

9.9 — Arrive parking lot and turn right on unnamed road. Soon bend left and then right and eventually parallel Amtrak corridor.

11.1 — Arrive Neptune Drive and climb over fence or go straight ahead on single track under power line.

11.3 — Bear right onto Sunrise Road. Pass tennis courts.

11.5 — Left on Neptune.

11.9 — Left on Nautilus, straight onto Anchorage Circle, bear slightly left on Bass Drive, left on Colony Road.

12.4 — Right on Mumford Cove Road.

12.6 — Bear left on Groton Long Point Road.

12.9 — Right on Marsh Road.

13.4. — Knock around Noank or follow this route. Right on Terrace, right on High, left on Spring, left on Pearl, right on Palmer which becomes Riverview, right on Main, left on Front, left on Ward.

14.6 — Right on Mosher Avenue.

14.7 — Right on Route 215/Elm Street.

17.2 — Arrive back at Mystic Drawbridge.

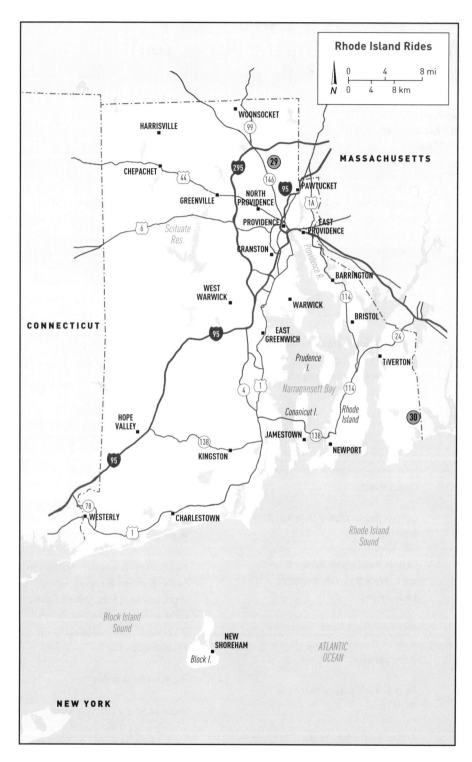

Rhode Island Rides

0 4 8 mi
0 4 8 km
N

WOONSOCKET
99

HARRISVILLE

MASSACHUSETTS

CHEPACHET

44   295   29

146   95   PAWTUCKET

GREENVILLE   NORTH
PROVIDENCE   1A

6   Scituate
Res.   PROVIDENCE   EAST
PROVIDENCE

CRANSTON

Providence R.

BARRINGTON

WEST
WARWICK   WARWICK   114

BRISTOL

EAST
GREENWICH   24

CONNECTICUT   95   Prudence
I.   TIVERTON

Narragansett Bay   114

4   1   Conanicut I.   Rhode
Island

HOPE
VALLEY   30

95   JAMESTOWN   138   NEWPORT

138   NEWPORT

KINGSTON

78
WESTERLY   CHARLESTOWN   Rhode Island
Sound

1

Block Island
Sound   NEW
SHOREHAM   ATLANTIC
OCEAN

Block I.

NEW YORK

RIGHT: THE STATUESQUE CONGREGATIONAL CHURCH AT THE HEAD OF
THE COMMON IN LITTLE COMPTON

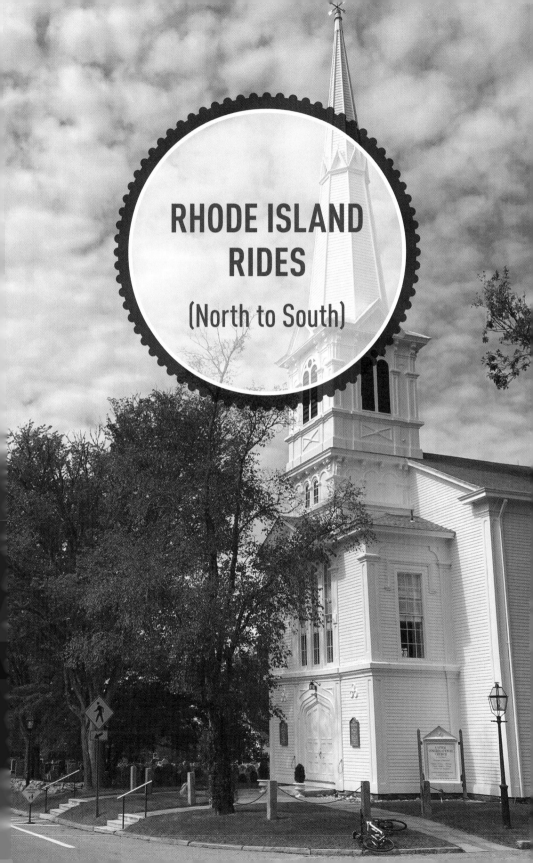

RHODE ISLAND RIDES

(North to South)

LOOKING SOUTH ALONG BLACKSTONE RIVER AT THE ASHTON MILL COMPLEX

29

Blackstone River Valley National Historic Park

Lincoln Villages of Albion, Ashton, and Lime Rock, Rhode Island

DISTANCE: 10.1 miles
ELEVATION GAIN: 434 feet
EASY

A surprisingly beautiful and historic bike trail in the midst of suburban, industrial, and commercial sprawl. Especially appealing for history buffs.

The Blackstone River Valley National Historic Park is the birthplace of the industrial revolution in the United States and is chock full of 17th- to 21st-century historically preserved places. This ride is a nice introductory sampler of the intriguing biking/history possibilities in this area.

The unique loopification challenge in urban areas is how to go one way on a bike path and create a different, appealing route back to your starting point. This avoids the out-and-back experience.

You'll see that this loop is a moderately successful solution to this problem. If you're cool with out-and-back then starting in Albion and heading up to Woonsocket or south to Valley Falls and back would be wonderful route options.

Start your ride at the Blackstone Bikeway parking area on School Street in Albion, one of the villages of Lincoln, Rhode Island. It's on the west bank of the Blackstone River, adjacent to a massive Highland Falls mill complex that now houses upscale condos. Jump on the trail heading south and quickly cross the river—great views, north and south. You'll be impressed by the design and elegance of the trail. It's recently paved and has attractive split rail fencing on the river side. You'll think, *Hey, someone really cares about creating a nicely crafted bike experience.* When you cross the river at the Ashton Mills complex, make sure you check out the Captain Wilbur Kelly house—the home of one of the early cotton mill entrepreneurs in the valley. The historic house museum is located between the river and the historic Blackstone Canal. Like the Erie Canal, the Blackstone Canal really was only commercially viable from the mid-1820s to the mid-1840s. The arrival of the railroad put the canals out of business. But the towpath for the canal now provides the route for much of the bike trail.

South from the Kelly house, the bike path is wedged on high ground beneath the sultry canal and the river, far away from traffic and sirens. It provides the same kind of time travel moment as the Battle Path in Minuteman National Park. Before crossing the river again, you'll turn right off the trail and head out through a parking area on a bikeway access road to Front Street. Now the questionable return route and the historical whiplash experiences commence.

HISTORIC KELLY HOUSE MUSEUM ALONG BLACKSTONE HERITAGE TRAIL

Head west on Front Street amidst commercial sprawl for 0.7 miles. Front Street becomes Great Street, you round a corner and poof, you're transported backward three centuries to the 1693 Eleazer Arnold house. How often do you come upon 17th-century buildings? You continue along, now in the Great Road Historic District, which includes the early 19th-century Moffett Mill, the Hannaway Blacksmith Shop, and the Hearthside House Museum. And this is surrounded by the preserved Chase Farm, one of the best-preserved examples of early 19th-century landscape in Rhode Island. When we were there a 17th-century replica of Salem, Massachusetts, was being constructed as a set for the filming of *Hocus Pocus 2*. This mile-long stretch of road is also

historic in that it is very narrow with no shoulder and lots of fast-moving traffic, which makes it hard to gawk at the cool historic buildings and meadows. But just after Hearthside, you bear right on Great Road while the main road turns left, and you're on a reasonably quiet country road.

Here's the aerobic section of the ride. You climb up over a 200-foot hill, start to descend the other side, and poof, back to the 17th century in the lost village of Lime Rock. Limestone quarrying was one of the first industrial enterprises in this area in the late 1600s and this village grew up around the quarries, which still operate today. Head past the village onto Wilbur Road if you want to see the quarries, then turn around, back through the village, and head north on Anna Sayles

BIKING SOUTH ALONG BLACKSTONE HERITAGE TRAIL BETWEEN RIVER AND CANAL

TREASURE HUNT: SOMEWHERE IN THE GREAT ROAD HISTORIC DISTRICT IN MIDDLE OF RIDE

Road. The rest of the route is securely 20th and 21st century.

Cross Route 116 on Old River Road, pass the high school and the library, cross 1-295, and take a quick right on Kirkbrae Road—solid suburbia. Kirkbrae becomes Timberland and then you'll take a left on Briarwood. Expending all that elevation you gained earlier, you'll transverse nicely tended lawns and pass a stunning hodgepodge of suburban architectural styles from ranches to colonials to mid-century moderns. When you arrive at the intersection with School Street, note the nondescript building on the right with the hair salon and the Azorean Kitchen. Right on School Street and you're back at your car in a flash.

DINING OPPORTUNITIES

The **Azorean Kitchen** wasn't open when we biked by, but this would be my choice for a post-ride lunch. How often do you get to try Portuguese cuisine? Codfish and potato croquettes, shrimp Mozambique, mussels with chouriço, and, my fave: Portuguese kale soup.

For more conventional fare, try **GottaQ Barbeque** in Cumberland just a mile from where you're parked. Not charming, but solid, hickory smoked meats. The Q-ban sandwich is particularly good. For old times' sake, have a draft of Narragansett Lager, made by one of the original New England microbreweries founded in 1890 that died and has been reborn in the past decade.

SWIMMING OPPORTUNITY

Also untested but promising are the two freshwater beaches in Lincoln Woods State Park. You passed an entrance on Great Road. There's a nice 4-mile loop around the lake that you could add to the middle of the ride. Reports of the swimming experience appreciated if you try it out.

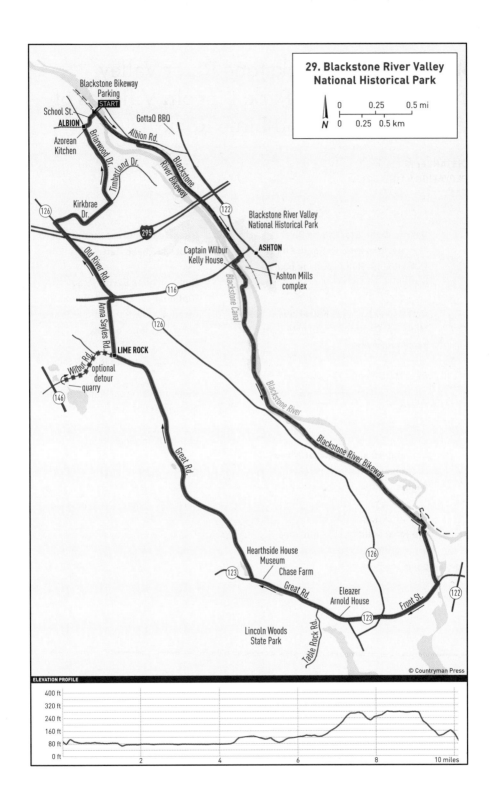

29. Blackstone River Valley National Historical Park

0   0.25   0.5 mi

N   0   0.25   0.5 km

Blackstone Bikeway Parking
START
School St.
ALBION
GottaQ BBQ
Albion Rd.
Azorean Kitchen
Briarwood Dr.
Timberland Dr.
Blackstone River Bikeway
Kirkbrae Dr.
126
295
122
Blackstone River Valley National Historical Park
Captain Wilbur Kelly House
ASHTON
Ashton Mills complex
Old River Rd.
116
126
Blackstone Canal
Anna Sayles Rd.
LIME ROCK
Wilbur Rd.
optional detour
quarry
146
Great Rd.
Blackstone River
Blackstone River Bikeway
Hearthside House Museum
Chase Farm
123
126
Great Rd.
Eleazer Arnold House
Front St.
122
Lincoln Woods State Park
Table Rock Rd.
123

© Countryman Press

ELEVATION PROFILE

400 ft
320 ft
240 ft
160 ft
80 ft
0 ft
2   4   6   8   10 miles

AT A GLANCE Blackstone River Valley National Historic Park: Lincoln Villages of Albion, Ashton, and Lime Rock

DISTANCE: 10.1 miles
ELEVATION GAIN: 434 feet
EASY

0.0	Park in at the Blackstone River Trail parking area on South Street in Albion, RI. Head south on bike trail.
1.6	Cross river and visit Kelly House Museum. Continue south between canal and river.
4.0	Depart trail and head south on access road toward Front Street.
4.3	Right on Front Street/Route 123.
5.1	Continue straight on what is now Great Street. Historic district begins.
5.3	Lincoln Woods State Park. (Optional additional 4-mile loop around Olney Pond. Access to pond beach as well.)
5.9	Bear right on Great Street, where Route 123 bears left.
7.6	Right on Anna Sayles Road. (Optional out and back detour through Lime Rock village to operating limestone quarry.
8.2	Cross 116 onto Old River Road.
8.9	Right on Kirkbrae which becomes Timberland Drive.
9.4	Left on Briarwood Road.
10.0	Right on School Street.
10.1	Arrive Blackstone trail parking.

The Farm Coast

Adamsville and Little Compton, Rhode Island; and Acoaxet, Massachusetts

DISTANCE: 17.2 miles
ELEVATION GAIN: 541 feet
EASY

A quietly hidden and surprising corner of New England. Verdant green meadows with miles of precise, well-crafted stone walls. A glimpse of the Gilded Age at Acoaxet beaches. Suitable for road bikes.

Let me introduce you to two villages that your grandmother might refer to as "dear." They're as close to traditional New England villages as it gets in Rhode Island. The first, your starting point, is Adamsville, just barely in Rhode Island, west of Westport, Massachusetts. You'll park in the big lot at the Barn Restaurant (more on this place later), but you might want to get caffeinated at Gray's Daily Grind, just a stone's throw from where you're parking, but over there in Massachusetts.

Leave the parking lot and turn right on Main Street and then quickly left on Colebrook Road. You'll be surprised at the steepness of this half-mile climb in this flat part of the world, but it's really the only hill on the loop. And it won't feel very back roads-y for the first couple of miles. This ride is designed to get the less pleasant parts of the ride out of the way first. It's woodsy and uninteresting until you bear left on Long Highway, right on Peckham Road, left onto East Main. By here, the traffic has quieted down and the farmed landscape has started to open up. You can tell this was once all old sprawling farms and now many have been sliced up into farm-y burbs. But there are still lots of farmstands with plump pumpkins, rosy-cheeked apples, corn, squash, and mums. You'll bend around on East Main, take a right on Simmons Road, and at about 5 miles arrive in Little Compton, a comfortable little village with a tall spired Congregational Church, a beautiful green, the aptly named Common's Lunch, a classic old hardware store, a cute nature preschool, and a tea room/arts cafe. You'll want to loll around and take a nap in the grass, but you have miles to go.

Head south on South of Commons Road. Now you'll see why the tourist marketing term for this area is "the Farm Coast." The verdant meadows are demarcated by miles of cleanly precise stone walls and there's a gentle windswept hush over the landscape. You'll pedal along straight allées of maples and locust trees arching over the roads, with views across fields down to marshy ponds. Now, lots of right angle lefts and rights—left on Brownell, left on Maple, right on Sisson, left on Long Highway, right on Pottersville, right on Mullen Hill, right on Old Harbor. Woods break up the meadows and you're starting to think, *Hey, I thought this was a coastal ride, where are*

ALONG THE COAST IN ACOAXET

the ocean views? Funny you should ask. Once you turn right onto Howland Road, you start to smell the salt air. You'll pass the tidy Acoaxet Chapel and almost think you'd like to go to a Sunday service here. And then finally you're at the beach. Grey shingled cottages abound. The signs are a mite unwelcoming. Members Only. Private Club. No Trespassing. Don't Even Think of Parking Here. No Beach Access. But the biking is beautiful along Atlantic Avenue with the beach on one side and dunes on the other.

You'll bemoan the fact that grandmother never left you one of these nice, weathered, multi-porched, beach places to you in her will. At Acoaxet Road take a right and bend around on potholed Beach Road. There's a Gilded Age stone manse on the left, but straight ahead is the raîson d'ètre of the ride. The Knubble, a massive outcropping of granite, rises oddly above the dune grass and beach plum with great views of the Westport River and Horseneck Beach across the way. Hard to resist the scramble up to the top. And surprisingly, there's a charming, bounded by granite slabs, little beach right here for a quick plunge now or later when you drive back.

Head back out Beach Road, take a right on Acoaxet, and it's a long straight shot back up along the Westport River. There's pretty Cockeast Pond and eventually you're hard by the salt marsh upper reaches of the river before you roll back into Adamsville. Wouldn't it be nice to live here? That cute two-bedroom white Cape on the left is on the market for a mere $915 thousand. But it's sure a nice place to visit.

DINING OPPORTUNITIES

Well, hard not to want to eat at **The Barn**, but it's one of the few breakfast-only

EXHILARATED RIDER ON TOP OF THE KNUBBLE

restaurants that I know of. Closes at noon during the week, 1 p.m. on weekends. So carb up before your ride, or do an early morning ride and get a late breakfast after. It's a rustic, two-story renovated barn, always crowded, serves all breakfast favorites—eggs benedict, blueberry pancakes, omelets, Johnny Cakes.

Around the corner is **Simmons Cafe** featuring local and organic foods. Innovative sandwich menu for takeout including gyros and black bean burgers. Ice cream too. Perhaps breakfast at The Barn before your ride and lunch at Simmons?

Or go back over to Little Compton for a sit-down lunch at **The Common's Lunch**. Classic chowders, eggplant fries,

TREASURE HUNT: FIND THIS COLORFUL WINDOW NEAR THE BEGINNING OR END OF THE RIDE

fish and chips. Cozy, vintage diner feeling with vinyl booths. A meal here would complete your time travel experience.

SWIMMING OPPORTUNITIES

That little pocket beach at **The Knubble** is really the bee's knees, especially in this highly privatized section of coast. Cozy, sandy, easy access. If you want a bigger, wider beach experience, there's **South Shore Beach**, a Little Compton public beach at the end of South Shore Road off of Brownell Road. Or for the really big state beach experience, head over into Massachusetts to **Horseneck Beach State Reservation**. Less chichi and exclusive, more dunes, bigger waves.

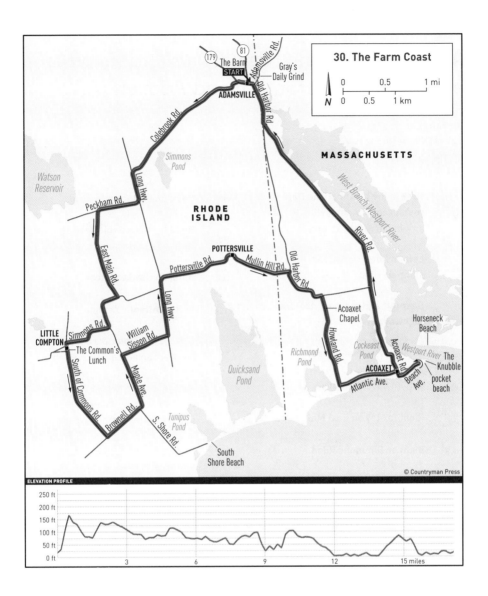

30. The Farm Coast

The Barn
START

Gray's
Daily Grind

ADAMSVILLE

MASSACHUSETTS

Colebrook Rd.

Simmons
Pond

Long Hwy.

Watson
Reservoir

Peckham Rd.

RHODE
ISLAND

West Branch Westport River

River Rd.

East Main Rd.

POTTERSVILLE

Pottersville Rd.

Mullin Hill Rd.

Old Harbor Rd.

Acoaxet
Chapel

Long Hwy.

LITTLE
COMPTON

Simmons Rd.

William
Sisson Rd.

The Common's
Lunch

Howland Rd.

Cockeast
Pond

Horseneck
Beach

Richmond
Pond

Quicksand
Pond

Acoaxet Rd.

Westport River

ACOAXET

The
Knubble
pocket
beach

South of Commons Rd.

Maple Ave.

Atlantic Ave.

Beach Ave.

Brownell Rd.

S. Shore Rd.

Tunipus
Pond

South
Shore Beach

© Countryman Press

ELEVATION PROFILE

250 ft
200 ft
150 ft
100 ft
50 ft
0 ft

3   6   9   12   15 miles

AT A GLANCE The Farm Coast: Adamsville and Little Compton, RI; and Acoxet, MA

DISTANCE: 17.2 miles
ELEVATION GAIN: 541 feet
EASY

0.0	Park in the big lot at The Barn restaurant in Adamsville, RI. Take a right onto Main Street.
0.2	Left on Colebrook Road. Only substantial climb.
1.5	Bear left and merge onto Long Highway.
2.2	Right on Peckham Road.
2.7	Left on East Main Road.
3.8	Right to stay on East Main Road.
4.3	Right on Simmons Road.
4.9	Arrive Little Compton. Continue south on South of Commons Road.
6.1.	Left on Brownell Road.
6.6	Left on Maple Road. then right on William Sisson Road and left on Long Highway.
8.6	Right on Pottersville Road.
9.5	Right on Mullen Hill Road and then right on Old Harbor Road.
10.8	Right on Howland Road.
11.9	Left on Atlantic Avenue.
12.6	At Acoaxet Road take a right and bend around onto Beach Road.
13.0	Arrive at The Knubble. Scamper up. Retrace your route back to junction with Atlantic Avenue.
13.4	Head north on Acoaxet Road and merge with River Road.
16.8	Merge onto Old Harbor Road.
17.3	Arrive Old Barn in Adamsville.

Acknowledgments

AUTHOR DAVID SOBEL AND HIS WIFE, JEN, ON A RIDE

My sincerest appreciation goes to my wife, Jennifer Kramer, my trusty sidekick and trail partner, the Dale Evans to my Roy Rogers. During bike season—late March to early November—we aspire to biking five times a week, and her commitment has helped us maintain this discipline. She's embarrassed that she's the model in lots of the photos in this book. She's also the pace-setter: Whereas I tend to bike at the leisurely pace of about 9 mph, when she's alone she trucks along at more like 13 mph. She's helped to plan new routes and refine old ones. She's been along for every pedal stroke of the way.

Two other biking sidekicks stood in for Jen on some occasions. Chris Hardee and I biked almost every Wednesday in the pandemic summer of 2021, to help taste test some new rides and critique route decisions. He is the other main photographic contributor in this book, and from him I have learned that "foreground is everything" and "don't place the subject in the center of the frame." He also advocated, "If you see the great picture, stop on the dime and take it right then." In other words, don't assume that a similarly good version will show up in the next few minutes—it doesn't.

Craig Stockwell, one of those 40- or 50-miles-a-day bikers, has been a downhill-skiing, skating, Nordic-skiing, hiking, and biking companion for decades. He consented to come down to my level and sample some new rides in and around his summer place in Waterford, Maine, and on a couple of lovely warm October days in Connecticut. Craig looks the part of a bicyclist—long and lean—so you'll see him in some of these photos as well.

If you're around Keene, New Hampshire, for some of these rides and you need bike maintenance, I recommend Norm's Ski and Bike Shop. Specifically, ask for Jeremy. We owe him a deep thanks for keeping all of our mountain, hybrid, and gravel bikes in good working order. And I appreciate his willingness to sometimes do on-the-spot fixes.

Thanks to the city of Keene, the state of New Hampshire, and the rest of the New England states for recognizing the important role bicycling plays in maintaining the quality of life in our corner of the country and for reducing the carbon footprint of the citizenry. There have been consistent improvements in bike infrastructure across the region—from the bike bridges in Keene to the urban biking lanes in Boston to the work of Portland Trails in Maine. Let's hope this book encourages you to explore all the country lanes, river roads, and lost villages tucked away in all the New England states.